ON THE FARM

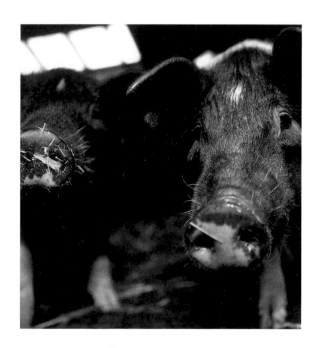

ON THE FARM

Jimmy Doherty

PHOTOGRAPHY BY CHRIS TERRY

EBURY
PRESS

CONTENTS

SUMMER how it all started

Nature is my passion – it's been my obsession for as long as I can remember. My parents moved from London to the beautiful Essex countryside when I was only three, but even then it felt as though a whole new world was opening up for me. We had a couple of acres filled with apple trees and stables stashed with junk to tinker through. My brother was potty about football but I would go off to spend hours outside to see what creatures I could discover or hunt for dead mice. Mum would often introduce me to people, who said what a nice little boy I was until I proudly presented them with a carrier bag of dead mice and maggots. I was so obsessed with finding out how nature worked that I soon moved on to collecting bones. When I was old enough, I kept ferrets, birds and tropical fish, and went to work at the local wildlife park. From then on, I never looked back. I studied hard and immersed myself in the world of insects and animals through A levels to a degree and even embarked on a PhD. But somehow, despite years of studying wildlife, I ended up working long days in London in an office job, catching the tube home late at night, exhausted and craving fresh air instead of city smoke and dust. I yearned to get back to a more wholesome way of life. So, last year, I made a momentous decision. It was time to take some risks, go the full Monty, pack up my London life and embark on a big adventure.

I think something in all of us wants to get back to nature and the pursuit of life's simple pleasures, whether it's growing your own vegetables or just walking barefoot along a beach. For most of us, lack of time and space means that the former might be a bit of a dream but if, like me, you love good food and care about what your family eats, consuming intensively farmed food can pose some problems. We are lucky enough to have no shortage of food in this country, but those bulging supermarket shelves have brought new and complex issues to consider. In the wake of BSE and foot-and-mouth disease more and more of us are starting to question food production, the movement of livestock and the over-use of pesticides, although few of us can do anything but shop in the local supermarket. Nevertheless, many of us worry where what we are buying comes from, what exactly is in it and why it can taste so bland despite all the attractive shapes and colours. How many months have the air-freighted veggies been stored before they hit the shelves? Why do we have a choice of watery and tasteless fruit and veg from all over the world, all year round, but few that are locally produced? Do you wonder where and how the insipid pre-packed chicken in your trolley was raised? Whether it has been fed antibiotics, pumped with preservatives, chemicals, water and goodness knows what else? All this brings with it serious health, environmental and economic issues that we confront every time we fill a trolley.

The problem, which started after the Second World War, is that food production has intensified beyond belief. In response to the pressures of consumer demand for cheap food, the farmer's accountant, and supermarket power and profit margin, it's now such a huge

OPPOSITE City life is fast-paced and exciting, so my friends found it hilarious when I said I'd had my fill of it and planned to escape to a pig farm. One year on, and much hard work later, they know I'm deadly serious.

mechanised monster that it has transformed our countryside into a factory. Massive wheat fields are without hedgerows, and livestock are kept in cramped conditions and fed on inappropriate diets – the aim is always to produce more and more, faster and faster, cheaper and cheaper. It's a destructive and ultimately self-defeating process. But it's not the only way. Think of European countries: food in Italy or France is some of the best around, partly because their inhabitants expect and demand high standards, and take pride in their produce, its quality and its regional character. But British food doesn't have to mean mass production and processed meals – we also have a great tradition of fine food.

With all this in mind, I decided it was time to trade tasteless, pre-packed, mass-produced pap for real food. I wanted to get back to basics. My aim was to harness and put into practice some of the more traditional British farming methods to produce good-quality, fresh, seasonal food as naturally as possible. And, of course, get a bit of the good life along the way. My grand idea was to live and work on a farm, raising animals and growing food. It seemed like the perfect way to put my theories to the test.

My plan was met with all sorts of reactions, but my girlfriend Michaela's was fairly typical. We'd met for the first time one and a half years earlier, whilst filming on Peter Gott's pig farm in Cumbria. I'd met Peter originally at Borough Market in Bermondsey, south London, where he was selling pork from his farm. We got talking and when I mentioned my interest in rare breeds and my dream of having a farm of my own one day, Peter invited me up to Cumbria to see his place and get some inspiration. Very quickly we became good friends. When Jamie was making his television series *Jamie's Kitchen*, about

teaching youngsters to become chefs, he wanted to take the students to a farm to give them a better understanding of where food comes from and how the good stuff is produced. I suggested that Peter's farm, where I was helping out at the time and learning the ropes, was the ideal place. Luckily for me, Michaela came along as part of the production team for Jamie's programme, and it was there, both of us standing ankle-deep in mud, that I first told her my dream of setting up my own pig farm like Peter's one day. She says she thought I was 'a bit weird' – well, I suppose it isn't exactly every young man's dream to run away from a London job to a pigsty. Despite my weirdness, she obviously saw something in me as we were still together when, eighteen months later, I told her I was going to take the plunge. Michaela was supportive all the way and knew that I could make it happen, but she had her worries. She could see that I was riding high on my grand ambitions and she didn't want me to fall to earth with an unpleasant bump when I had to face the realities that it would all entail.

Most of my friends pointed out that the average age of a farmer was probably about seventy, or asked why, out of all the different farms I could set up, I was keen on stinking pigs. My parents were supportive but were worried I wasn't experienced enough or very well prepared and I guess most people thought it was just a pipedream. So when I actually gave up my job and announced I was looking for a farm, there was a universal gasp of 'Ohmigod, he's actually going to do it!' Then the local media got wind of an Essex boy looking to start a farm with rare-breed Essex pigs and suddenly it became a big story. Now I really had to do it – so off I went, in the spring of 2003, on a nationwide search for the right farm to rent. The pressure was on now, and I threw myself into my project, determined to make it work.

Finding the farm

My first plan was a farm in Devon – how fantastic to be in the countryside and near the surf. Amazing! But I had no idea how or where to start looking, so I called upon my now friend and mentor in all things piggy, Peter Gott. In true farming style he had a mate who owed him a favour and after a phone call I suddenly had a companion to show me round the spectacular Devonshire countryside. Chris Muir (whose family used to be in pig farming) and I took off for a week, driving from Holsworthy to Plymouth under the clear spring skies. It was a whirlwind tour of some remote, tucked-away places, where we talked to some lovely people, as well as a few gently nutty types who had obviously not had any visitors for a while. But despite wonderful scenery, fields filled with new lambs, and masses of snowdrops, nowhere really captured my imagination. Some of the farms looked perfectly good, but there was always a hitch: a farmer who wanted to continue occupying a proportion of his land, or a location that wasn't quite right.

My farm would have to make money – that was paramount, and it meant that my

OPPOSITE Finding the perfect farm took several months, and at first only I could see its perfection. Where others saw neglect and decay, I saw once-lovely buildings and fertile land bursting with potential.

criteria for finding the perfect patch were based upon the market. The farm needed to be a place where it was possible for my rare-breed livestock to range freely, where I could set up a farm shop to sell the produce they generated, and be accessible for people to come and fill big bags with fresh farm produce. Easy enough, you might think, but I ended up searching all over the UK. I even advertised in local papers for suitable land. From Bath to the New Forest to Oxford I went, often riding around paddocks on the back of a tractor with some drunken old boy in charge of the wheel. I must have looked at almost thirty farms. A lot of them had fairly modern buildings and were pretty much in full working order, so they would have been easy to take on; others were stunning. Michaela fell in love with one in tip-top condition on a National Trust estate in Herefordshire – it had four barns for animals and a fourteenth-century house surrounded by a moat. But, for me, it just didn't compare to what I was about to discover.

It was a day that had started just like many others around that time. The spring morning had dawned bright and sunny and I was off on a trip to see yet another farm. I'd spotted Pannington Hall Farm advertised in a Suffolk paper but I'd seen so many places that by now I was fairly pessimistic and I didn't hold out much hope. That was, until I took a sharp turn off a bustling A-road and found myself in a tree-lined lane. The approach to the farm was pretty dramatic: the lane dipped into woodland as we passed a little old cottage and drove towards the entrance gates in the distance. I could see a figure that

seemed to be waiting for us there. It turned out to be Simon, the owner of the farm.

As I slammed the car door, I took in the view. The fields and paddocks were studded with bluebells and daffodils, but it was easy to see that rabbits were the only things that had turned over the soil in years. There was a large paddock on one side, woodland on the other, a lovely old farmhouse that looked like it had seen better days, and a crumbling ancient tractor shed. Everything had been left to run wild and fall into disrepair, but, as I looked round, I couldn't help but see how the open fields might have looked years ago and how the buildings must have bustled with life, even though we now had to force our way through weeds just to get into them. The farmhouse had been stripped bare by squatters; the old barn, once the longest thatched building in Suffolk, was cold and ghostly, its doors flapping in the breeze, its roof smashed and its courtyard redundant.

As we wandered around and Simon showed me the farm buildings with their charred timbers and tileless roofs, I pointed out the woodland. 'Who owns that?' I asked and, to my disbelief, Simon was happy to throw in the woods with the rental. Now things were really getting interesting. The woodland was magical. Wild garlic carpeted the forest floor and smelt pungent as we trudged our way across the earth and fallen branches on our way down to the tiny stream at the woodland's edge. I was growing more excited every moment – I could envision pigs in the wood, rubbing their backs against the bark and foraging in the undergrowth. I could see beyond the brambles and bracken to a flourishing wood nurturing wildlife and livestock, and a farm restored to its past glory. Yes – this was it!

I wasn't put off by the state of the farm. The fact that it hadn't been touched for twenty years and that its former owners had left because their business was no longer viable really represented the decline of British farming. I knew that turning the farm round would be extremely hard work, but carving it back out of the wilderness meant that I would be able to create something new and unique, rather than having to work within someone else's structure, and I was certain I could make the farm into a successful commercial venture while staying true to my ideals of getting back to nature. As soon as I'd made the decision that this was the place for me, things really started to slot into place. I discovered that this part of the world was true Essex pig country and traditionally home to some of the best of the breed that this good Essex boy was hoping to keep. It turned out that one of the local farmers near by, used to keep some of the best Essex pigs in the country.

I signed the lease feeling that this was the start of something exciting and it was all meant to be. The next thing to do was to show Michaela . . .

The weather had really started to heat up the day we went to visit. I remember Michaela and myself heading off in the car – windows down, music blaring – and thinking she'd have to love the farm on a day like this. We turned into the lane and it looked incredible. The young spring shoots had unfurled, the trees were heavy with lush green

OPPOSITE **Like the rest of the farm, the woodland had long been neglected, but it was the perfect place for pigs to forage.**

RIGHT Michaela and I: I am full of enthusiasm and big ideas, whilst Michaela has a practical streak that keeps my feet on the ground.

leaves and dappled sunlight rippled their shadows on the lane. It looked more like rural Italy than Suffolk.

'This is going to be amazing,' Michaela muttered excitedly, as we swooped past the gates. 'Wow, it's beautiful!' she gasped, as the farmhouse stood proudly in front of us in the distance. As we pulled to a stop, she started to talk about how great the position was, how the location was really impressive. She hopped down from the car seat and saw the great chestnut and magnolia trees, still impressed. But her face started to change as we walked towards the farmhouse and she realised it was derelict, and saw how the land had been left to deteriorate so badly. We went over to the tractor shed and by now she was looking at me like I was completely crackers. I launched into my explanation of what we could do to the place and how we could set up the farm shop here – I was probably talking a million miles an hour as usual, arms gesticulating wildly. 'This is where the counter will be,' I remember saying, and Michaela stopped me, laughing. 'Jim, there's nothing here but huge holes in the roof and earth on the floor!' She was the voice of reason. Michaela had absolute faith that I could turn the farm around, but she never lost sight of how much work there was to be done and how much money it would take. How right she was. But I was determined – this place was going to be my farm.

Work begins at Jimmy's farm

The beginning of summer 2003 was the real start of my big adventure. After seven months of searching for the right farm. I'd been living in Walthamstow, east London, or with my parents, and now I was ready to move to the farm full time, even though there was nowhere to live as such – the farmhouse wasn't fit for habitation unfortunately, even though I had some plans for it eventually. I'd be camping out for a while, until I managed to arrange something more permanent, but that didn't matter. My dream of owning a farm was finally coming true and I'd have happily slept in the trees if that's what it took to be there. But I also had to stay realistic and I had worked out a plan for what I could achieve in a year, by which time the farm would have to be a profitable business or I'd be in serious trouble. With hard work and a bit of help, I was confident I could do it. Summer would be devoted to getting the farm into some kind of working order; once it was cleared and renovated, we could move in the livestock, starting small with chickens and moving up towards the final goal: pigs. By the autumn I hoped to have a solid herd of pigs and the first litters of the piglets on the way so that we could begin to generate produce for the farm shop – which, of course, would also need designing, building and kitting out. Then there was the website, the mail-order business and the whole process of learning how to make and sell our pork products. When I thought about it all at once, it seemed like a crazy amount to achieve in such a short time; the best way was to set short-term goals and concentrate on getting those under my belt. Right now, that meant good old-fashioned hard work. . .

The first day I started work on the farm was momentous – it felt like the beginning of a great adventure. It was going to be a lot of hard labour that I couldn't manage alone, so I recruited my friends Asa and Rick to help me kick things off. I guess you could call Rick my right-hand man. We'd met at Coventry University, where he was studying for a degree in Environmental Science and I was working, supervising practicals and leading tutorial groups. During the times we spent in the lab together, I found out that Rick was keen to change his life too and that, among other things, he'd trained many years ago as a butcher. It was inevitable that we ended up bouncing ideas around and dreamt about setting up a farm. We kept in touch after the course, but I don't think Rick could quite believe it when, after months and months of talking, I finally called him to take him up on his offer of help, now that I actually had a farm. He was full of enthusiasm but I'm not sure he knew exactly what was in store.

We were about to start some serious physical work in what was officially the hottest summer since 1976. I rocked up to the farm in the truck with Rick and my scruffy little terrier Cora, and we could hardly believe we were in England: the vehicle kicked up huge swirls of dust where the earth had got so dry and all around we could hear crickets and grasshoppers – it was just like being on holiday. The first thing to do was the back-breaking work of ribbing – clearing the land of the rubbish and overgrowth that was strangling it. Twenty years of neglect had meant that the land had gone wild and was almost buried in nettles, bracken, long grass and dead trees and, boy, did I hear about it! We set to work early to try and get as much of the debris cleared as possible and see what was really there before the heat of the sun slowed us down. I'd come armed with the best petrol-powered strimmer I could find in my local DIY store, thinking 'This will do the job' – but we soon made our way through two or three of those. The vegetation was so thick that I would suddenly hit some railings and – snap! Another one would bite the dust. The foliage was so high that we discovered a dormant 6-foot high petrol pump that used to fuel the tractors on the farm; it had been completely invisible. The sun beat down on our backs as we cursed the lightweight strimmers, fixing their troublesome belts back on again and again but we cleared enough to discover an orchard and some gates. The orchard had grown into a mini woodland that we had to hack our way through with axes. By the end of the day our bodies ached, our faces were covered in a film of sweat and dirt, and our hands were pulsating with blisters. We were thankful when Asa turned up just in time to lift our spirits.

Asa and I had stayed close ever since we'd met at one of my mate Jamie's book signings where he was a security guard. I'd offered him a cuppa and he reckoned it was the nicest gesture anyone had ever made to him at work, bless him! We ended up going out for a few beers and quickly became good mates, eventually sharing a flat in the East End of London. I thought Asa's training in the Royal Marines would come in pretty useful on the farm where strength is always an asset and he's always keen to help out, muck in and provide a few laughs along the way. And, boy, did we need his humour to keep us going!

To mark the occasion and thank the guys for their help, I decided to treat them to a Jimmy-style barbecue that first night on the farm. I'd bought a huge salmon and some big juicy steaks in a cool box, along with some beers, and as evening approached I set about preparing dinner. First of all we got the fire going, using the wood from one of the ash trees we'd had to fell. Next, I thrust some plastic bottles filled with water into the raging fire to bring their contents to the boil. The guys though I'd gone bonkers and that the plastic would melt, but five years in the Territorial Army had taught me otherwise – the cold water, which is at a lower temperature than the fire round it, keeps the plastic cool up until the last minute when you whip it out, just in time. It's an old bushman's trick, and a good one. I gathered some tiles that had fallen off the roof of one of the outbuildings to cook the fish on. Then I mixed up some marinade in a plastic food bag so that it didn't get dirty and smothered the steaks before sticking them on the fire. I made some flat bread in pretty much the same way, mixing the dough in a plastic bag before cooking it over the fire on sticks. What a feast! You really should give it a go before resorting to the standard burger-in-a-bun – see my recipe on page 210. That night we should have slept like babies after our exertions, but I made the mistake of sleeping in the truck while the boys did the sensible thing and slept in a tent. The next day was hard enough, without aching from sleeping all twisted up.

OPPOSITE **Twenty years of rampant growth had to be cut back to reveal the true nature of the farm. We removed tons of rubbish, but also made some interesting finds, including a petrol pump and a well.**

Our mission the next morning was to carry on clearing some of the undergrowth. I thought that it would be fitting for Asa to rage war on the Japanese knotweed with a machete: it's a tough and persistent weed but with Asa being an ex-Royal marine, I reckoned it stood no chance. The weed was a formidable enemy, though, and the work nearly killed him. Next, Asa, Rick and I set to work slashing even more foliage. Asa probably felt as though he was back in the jungle, Brunei or somewhere, but the work really took its toll on all of us, and it was only just beginning.

It took a good few weeks to begin to see what the land really looked like underneath years of rambling vegetation. It was gruelling work but we had to clear the old to set up the new. I soon got fed up with the DIY-store strimmers and invested £600 on some proper kit – rule number one: you need the right tools for the task – and a pretty good job we did, considering the enormity of the undertaking. To give you an idea, it took Rick and me a week or so to cut back enough vegetation to reveal that we had a well on the farm. We also tackled the foliage around the farm buildings and revealed yet more work to be done – new walls, new roofs, new doors, and a lot of TLC would be needed to make them useable. But these were next on our list. In the meantime I needed to think about fixing some permanent accommodation – camping out on the farm wouldn't be

quite so pleasant when winter came. So, in the midst of all the labour, I was also constantly on the phone, trying to organise water, electricity and drains to be set up on the farm, and I started to search for some mobile homes to buy.

For weeks, Rick and I lived in a tent, cooked on a camp-fire, and worked all seven days of the week in the heat, with visits from Michaela and Rick's wife Lynn at weekends to see how we were getting on and lend a hand. It was fantastic to be outdoors, working on the land. We soon forgot about our city lives despite the tough labour and the unforgiving weather. Our reward was a jungle shower at the end of every day. We'd fill up plastic bottles with water from the well and stick them in the sun each morning, so that they would heat up through the day. Then we'd tie an empty sandbag round two trees to form a kind of tube – our shower cubicle. You would stand inside it, and pour down warm water from a large plastic bottle over your head. We'd take turns in the makeshift shower – it was amazing, and made me feel like running around naked.

We developed a great respect for the land and there was something very rewarding about trying to return it to its former glory. Although we could see how the land used to be laid out, we didn't know too much about the history of the farm until we bumped into old Matt one afternoon. Matt has known the farm for just about as long as he can remember. He was walking his dog on the public footpath one day and got a real shock seeing us there, working away. We stopped for a chat, patted his pooch and asked the old boy all about the history of the farm. He told us that the Wilson family had travelled down from the Mull of Kintyre to Suffolk in 1927 to set up an arable dairy farm stocked with Shorthorns, finally settling on this site in 1945. Matt started as a farmhand here in 1945, a week before his fifteenth birthday, and spent years working on the Wilson land and feeding their cows – the milk they produced was sold around Europe. He remembers the farmhouse bustling with life and the barns filled with cows being milked by the local women. During the war Land Girls were called in to increase the production of bottles to be rationed off locally, and the farm was even bombed during the war. Matt had seen it all and when we invited him back on to the land for another look around, his face was aglow. He said we'd 'turned the clocks back' and he was 'fifteen again'. The farm had remained largely untouched since the Wilsons were forced to pack up and leave in 1988. He was pleased someone was finally working the farm, although he wished I'd managed it fourteen years earlier. We did too, except I may have been a bit young to be allowed my own farm back then.

Rick, Asa and I pushed on with the work until the spring bank holiday, when, almost ready to drop, we took a brief but well-deserved break. While Rick spent some time with his wife and kids, I decided to visit the Suffolk Show for some farming inspiration.

The Suffolk is one of the most important agricultural shows in the country and a key event for farmers, so I was keen to be part of it and see what I could find out about rare-

ABOVE Weeks of back-breaking work during the hottest summer for years was a real endurance test for everyone involved. A cold beer or three at the end of the day was heaven.

breed pigs. It's also just a few miles from the farm, so I arrived on the opening day in no time, amid an atmosphere of high excitement and thousands of people. It was early but all sorts of things were already happening: there were terrier races, horses pulling traditional machinery in the paddocks, and people selling just about everything imaginable from plants to clothing – you could even buy a tractor. There was a fantastic food hall, too, a vast marquee filled with hundreds of stalls selling all types of produce, along with smoked and cured meats, hog roasts and sausages (to name a few of my favourites), which made grabbing a bite at lunchtime a mind-boggling and mouth-watering experience. Afterwards, as the sun blazed through the clouds and families turned up in their droves, I went in search of the Taste of Anglia stand. Taste of Anglia is a body of small independent food producers from the local area who pool their collective experiences of producing quality food for the consumer market. The Suffolk show explores many different aspects of British farming, from sheep shearing to keeping pigs, and it's all done with live commentary and entertaining demonstrations. I turned up just in time to see cows being milked and kids patting the heads of calves. But the showing of the different breeds of animals was my favourite event, so I headed for the main ring, passing a dog show to rival Crufts and two further marquees the size of aircraft hangars filled with flowers and nursery trade exhibits on my way. At the ring, a group of farmers in crisp white coats proudly showed cattle, sheep, horses and pigs that had all been washed, groomed and prepared to perfection. It was great to see all the different breeds of animal, from Tamworth and Gloucester Old Spot pigs to Suffolk Punch horses, and hear the farmers pass on information about what had been happening on their farms that year as they waited for their turn in the ring. It was a real community event. I ended up meeting some lovely characters who bred the livestock, and I relished finding out more about Essex pigs from a real Irish character, Vaughan Byrne, Mr Pig himself, who let me glean a bit of his pig-breeding wisdom. That day really bolstered my enthusiasm for farming and taught me a lot. I even came home armed with some eggs from Ancona chickens (a rare breed), which I planned to give to a friend to hatch for me.

I realise that I keep harping on about rare breeds, and some people might wonder what all the fuss is about. Surely a pig is a pig and a chicken is a chicken? Well, not exactly. Let's take the pig as an example. The modern pig is a product of intensive farming that has been developed by the farmer responding to the pressures of the consumer and the accountant. In other words, it is a commercial breed that has been developed to have bigger litters and grow faster than is natural, so that pork can be produced at super speed. The trouble with this is, as with anything in life, if you cut corners, you lose something. In this instance, it's flavour. While these pigs produce more pork, it's of relatively poor quality compared to the old or rare breeds such as the Essex or Saddleback. These rare-breed pigs have been bred for a more traditional way of life: they are usually kept outdoors, rather than in a fattening house, so that they can range freely; they have smaller litters and take a lot longer to mature, which means their flavour is enhanced because their muscles have longer to develop. They forage for their own food and are good at looking after themselves and their young. Because these pigs have been

OPPOSITE AND BELOW The Suffolk Show is one of the most important agricultural shows in the country – an opportunity to show and examine fine livestock, to spend time with like-minded people and to catch up with the latest farming news.

bred for may years in their natural environment, their natural immunity is very high. By contrast the commercial pig has been so over-bred that many of these good traits have been lost and as a result they're more susceptible to illness and loss. So, if you're willing to put quality before cost and quantity, rare breeds make prefect sense. Fantastic free-range sausages and pork that are produced in a welfare-friendly way may cost you a little more, but the taste alone is well worth the extra pennies. The proof is in the bacon.

Before we could think about buying our own livestock, Rick and I had to press on with getting the farm geared up for the animals' arrival. Having cleared away the bulk of the vegetation, we could now see the lie of the land and it was glorious. There was something awesome about standing back in the mid-summer sunshine, hands on hips, absolutely exhausted and covered in muck, and thinking, 'Blimey, we did that!' But we tried not to get too excited. Setting up the farm felt like a continual rollercoaster ride – it would take ages to feel like we were making progress, slowly shunting up the tracks, then we'd reach the top, elated, thinking we'd achieved something, only to hurtle down the other side to tackle the next big obstacle or task. And all the while, despite how much we achieved, we were also aware that the clock was ticking. We had to get the farm prepared for the animals so that they could settle in and have everything they needed for winter, and, just as importantly, we had to get the farm shop into shape so that the farm could start paying for itself.

The next step

Once the land was clear of the worst of the vegetation, our next task was to think about

ABOVE I always wanted to have a mixed farm and that meant poultry too!

where to put up our fencing. It may sound obvious but this is not something you can go into willy-nilly. A farm is usually laid out in a particular way for a particular reason – so that it flows ergonomically. If you just whack in a gate here and pop in a fence there, you could end up making a right mess and a lot of extra legwork in your day-to-day running of the farm. For this reason, some sites take a couple of generations to get right, the farmers making an odd change here and there every few years. Well, time was a luxury we didn't have, so we had to think hard about where the pigs and chickens would live, as well as every conceivable point of access, and get it right first time, although we tried to build in some flexibility for the farm to develop and change organically, as no doubt it would. Once our plans were finished, we got to work with the sturdiest posts and strongest barbed wire we could find. I was soon calling up a mate to borrow a post-basher machine – the job was just too vast, the sun too blazing and some of the earth too tough to consider bludgeoning each one into the ground with a mallet. Sometimes you just have to accept your own, very human limitations and get a machine to help you get the job done. The machinery was a godsend but we still put hours into the back-breaking task. I wanted the pigs and chickens to run as free as possible, so we had to ensure there were no obvious escape routes; if we missed a tiny hole, the animals could end up on someone else's land or, worse, on the A-road to Ipswich. But we were, after all, amateurs at this particular task. In our defence, it is pretty solid but there is no hiding the fact that the whole long line of stock fencing that runs down to the railway track is actually upside down, it should probably be another foot into the ground and when I say line, it sure weaves a wiggly one. I guess it's a constant reminder that some things this summer were a learning experience.

Building walls and repairing roofs are jobs you probably wouldn't associate with farming but that was the reality of life on the farm this summer. All these things had to be done, and fast. Luckily, some people who came to help out were skilled craftsmen. One of the first to arrive was Dolly. Dolly was his nickname and I still don't know his first name but Dolly was how he introduced himself and Dolly he has stayed. We met one balmy afternoon when Dolly was out bird-watching on the public footpath, as he has done regularly for fifteen years. There he was, binoculars poised, motionless by the hedgerows, as I finished off yet another line of fencing. I went up to say hello and, a bit breathless from the work, I explained what we were doing at the farm and that I needed a bit of a hand. Dolly told me he had seen the farm change from being a flourishing business to an overgrown, dilapidated and somewhat sad site, and would be delighted to lend a hand. To my absolute joy, he also said he was a handyman and could help me out. Now that's what I wanted to hear!

When you're working in an office in the city, you think, 'Blimey, when I'm stuck out in the sticks, how will I find anyone to muck in?' But it's funny how things work out – some people seem to pop up out of nowhere, and the rest of the time you can rely on the good old country tradition of calling in favours from other farmers and offering whatever you can in return, be it lending a hand on their land, or just giving them some of your freshly made sausages or a simple bag of tasty apples. But before we could produce anything to trade we had some walls to build.

Dolly set about digging up all of the old bricks from the buildings around the farm, which now lay scattered and useless. He carefully cleaned off the salvaged bricks and set to work with my brother Danny to build a wall in the old courtyard to keep the pigs behind. Even Michaela helped out at the weekend, despite her complete lack of brick-laying experience, pointing the wall with mortar as it went up. Within two days it was complete. What a team! There were still the other outbuildings to patch up, roofs to tile and loose boxes to make good, but it was an encouraging start.

But hang on a minute – it was all very well sorting out accommodation for the animals, but what about us? Camping out had been brilliant fun but we knew it would be a different story when the weather turned, so I pushed on with trying to find a couple of suitable mobile homes for Rick and myself. I had made hundreds of calls, responding to free ads, phoning up as many caravan companies as I could find and looking at countless different styles of mobile home on the net – I was becoming something of an expert – but I hadn't been able to find the right ones. The trouble was, most of them were just so chintzy. They'd been decked with faux period features and floral furnishings, and some even looked like the inside of a pub. I was on a mission to find wide berths, with lots of space and a plain interior. It wasn't easy. Eventually I found a brand that supplied almost all of those three elements and I ended up settling on two mobile homes for £10,000 from Sambeck Caravans. The only catch was that mine had a Barbie pink interior – not really my sort of thing at all, but to be honest, by this time it was the last of my worries.

I didn't imagine that getting our new homes on to the farm would pose yet another problem, but what a day . . . Rick and I had woken up that sunny morning dreaming of life's little luxuries. Over a camp-fire we made a cuppa and talked about how great it would be just to flick on a light switch, grab a cold beer from the fridge, sit at a table to eat dinner and on the sofa to listen to the radio. Comfort aside, this was a big step and we were very excited. We could now live permanently on site and finish making it secure, allowing us to buy our first livestock. We eagerly awaited the arrival of the delivery men as Michaela, her older brother Sean and Michaela's mate Des rolled up to witness the big event.

We soon heard the deep rumble that only a 38-ton lorry can make and it was coming from the top of the lane. But just as we started to get excited, we heard it stop with an enormous expulsion of steam. Without a word we all hurtled out of the farm gates to see what was happening. And there it was. The giant white truck with 'Sambeck Caravans' emblazoned on the side was towing the first mobile home, but it was just too huge and its roof had become firmly wedged into the overhanging trees. We raced back to the farm to grab chainsaws and hedge strimmers. Des, Rick and I climbed up into the trees to break off branches and we finally set the vehicle free, congratulating ourselves on a close shave. The lorry set off down the lane to the next big dip and, although it had looked like plain sailing, it promptly got stuck again! What a nightmare – we'd had a downpour that morning and the earth had become a quagmire. Michaela, Sean and Des ran back to the farm to grab shovels and we all set to work digging behind the wheels, the delivery guys grabbing a spade each to join us and help. The driver fired up the engine and the truck crept forward only to get its wheels jammed in the bog again. Every few yards this would happen and two hours of creeping and shovelling, creeping and shovelling passed before the lorry even got close to the farm gates. Finally, in despair, one of the truck drivers headed back to his depot to pick up a tractor and pull the lorry out of trouble. Though grubby and shattered, we still found the energy to jump up and down on the back of the tractor like kids on a hotel bed, to jolt the lorry out of the mud. Hours later, wearing caked mud like camouflage and standing there sweaty, we happily watched the first mobile home being lifted into place. But that was only one down and there was still one to go.

The second lorry arrived soon after and we all prayed that the process would be a bit smoother. The driver had obviously been told of the previous shenanigans and was taking no chances. After warning us to stand well back, he put his foot down and moved

OPPOSITE **Despite the rickety outbuildings and the makeshift shower, the farm absorbed me heart and soul. But even I had to admit that the comfort of a caravan was preferable to bivouacking round a camp-fire.**

all 38 tons and the weight of the mobile home swiftly into place at 40 miles per hour, mud flying in his heavy tracks. The guys and the truck drivers worked so hard that day – I don't know what might have happened had they not put so much welly into getting things sorted. Rick was supposed to go home to his family in Nuneaton that night, and the rest of the gang were planning to leave early, but everyone felt obliged to hang around after all the effort we'd made that day. We also wanted to celebrate, so we wired up the stereo, threw some fish on the barbecue and cracked open some champagne, falling about laughing at the chintzy decor in our new homes, but relieved they had finally arrived in one piece.

We now had electricity, water and decent shelter on site; we fitted our own drainage and a septic tank and we were away. Michaela started to do all she could to make the caravan feel like home when she visited at weekends. She was on a mission to grow a garden so the farm didn't 'look like a caravan park'. The problem was, as with every project on the site, she'd have to start from scratch. Undaunted, Michaela started to dig up the nettles and weeds on the patch of land outside our new front doors, while Rick and I continued to press on clearing the woodland and repairing the farm buildings. One day the barns and dairy would keep our pigs dry and fat, but before then, we needed to prepare winter bedding for the animals too.

It may seem strange to be thinking about winter at the height of summer, but with nature, you have to get organised for the frosty months pretty early on. You just know that you'll come unstuck if you don't sort things out in time – a bit like a squirrel nervously storing up nuts. Bedding for the animals is no exception. The world of farming is well aware of this and if, come winter, you haven't gathered enough straw in the summer harvest, you pay a real premium for it later because by then everyone wants it and the stores are depleted. So now, after four months of hard graft, we had the enclosures ready and I'd bought some animal feed, but we needed to sort out some bedding before we could buy the livestock. We had already bought a small amount of straw locally, but the farm next door was about to start cutting a load in their fields, so I asked if they could bundle it into small bales for me to buy. 'Great,' I thought. 'Couldn't be easier.' The bales were next door, they were nice and small and would be easy to handle. Well, not quite . . .

Rick and I got up at 5am the next morning to start bringing the bales round to the barn. The weather was beautiful, the fields were golden, but it was back-breaking, monotonous work. We had to pick up one bale, dust flying everywhere and sticking to our faces because we were so hot and sweaty, followed by wafts of stray bits of straw. We then had to take the bale to the truck and stack it up to be transported to the barn. This process was repeated until the truck was full. We than had to drive the truck round to the barn and finally re-stack all the bales in the barn. Back and forth we went, hundreds of

OPPOSITE Friends pitched in and helped us create a garden outside the caravan, even though the ground was little more than a weed-filled dustbowl.

times, and I soon wished we'd asked for fewer, larger bales. Rick and I worked relentlessly, without a break, but it wasn't until nine o'clock that evening that we unloaded the last of the bales. We felt as though we'd never stand up straight again! Worst of all was the realisation that the truck ended up with more straw in it than the barn. But it was great to have straw to sit on, a warm summer's evening to recuperate and the knowledge that we were a step closer to realising our dream.

The first animals arrive

It was time to get the first animals on to the farm and I couldn't wait. Chickens seemed the best livestock to plump for first; they're low maintenance and pretty much look after themselves, so they're a nice, gentle way to start keeping animals. And, of course, fresh eggs are fantastic. So off I went to see an old mate of mine, Animal Mark, who lives in Leicestershire. He's kept chickens for years on his allotment and I'd heard that he was about to sell some off to make way for a new batch. Anything that Mark had to sell had to be good because Animal Mark is, as his name might suggest, animal mad. In fact, he's a lab technician at Coventry University and was responsible for breeding animals for observation when I was there. He used to sneak his own pets into the department, so that when students came to study reptiles and amphibians, he'd have snakes and tarantulas to show them alongside the regulation frogs and toads. Their faces used to be a picture – but not half as good as Mark's when his tarantulas escaped from the lab one day and made their way down the corridors. You could see him panicked, his face as white as his lab coat, stamping his feet, trying to catch them!

LEFT The truck makes its way to the barn with a delicately balanced load of hay. It took dozens of trips to get enough for our needs.

OPPOSITE Looks easy, doesn't it? But lifting, stacking, unloading and re-stacking hundreds of bales is one of the most exhausting jobs I've ever done.

I ended up buying a job lot of twelve Warrens and Light Sussex chickens from Mark to start off with. It didn't matter that some of them were more than four years old, which is way past their best laying date. The main aim of the exercise was to test the fox population before increasing the numbers and breeds. To my relief, the foxes didn't seem very interested in the birds, so before long I was able to add to the flock. I bought some Black Rocks, a popular egg-laying breed, and went back to my mate who'd hatched the Anconas and Silkies (even more rare breeds) from the eggs I'd bought at the Suffolk Show.

The reasons for keeping rare-breed chickens are similar to the principles for rearing rare-breed pigs. The Warrens I bought from Mark are a commercial breed, the type of chicken that lays the eggs that you buy in the supermarket. Like most battery hens, they are bred to be egg-making machines. They reach their peak of production after the first year and, soon afterwards, when they pass their egg-laying date, they just about drop down dead with exhaustion. They're like a light that burns bright and flickers out fast. As they are usually bred and kept indoors in cramped conditions, they do not develop physically, so their only eating use would be to boil up the carcass for good chicken stock. The Light Sussex chickens are an altogether different species; they've been kept as a dual-purpose breed since Roman times, meaning that they are good for eating as well as for producing tasty eggs, and because they have been bred to suit an actual way of life, they are more of a slow burner. Like rare-breed pigs, rare-breed chickens have great disease resistance, they look after themselves and their chicks, find their own food and rarely need feeding in the summer months, aside from a few kitchen scraps to bolster the diet they glean from a free-range lifestyle. They lay fewer eggs, but they carry on laying for much longer. This goes for our Anconas and Silkies too. You may not get the quantity of eggs that battery hens offer, but there's a way around that – keep more chickens!

BELOW One of the first chickens I bought to start a laying flock.

So why keep chickens at all? Let me tell you, I'd recommend it to anyone. This summer, they brought life to the farm and were a big attraction. Aside from a ready supply of farm-fresh eggs and meat, they were a constant source of amusement. Believe me, if you keep chickens, you'll end up giving them names and chatting away to them as they cluck back at you and make you laugh out loud with their antics. They're highly intelligent and have their own individual personalities, which is all part of the fun. If you're thinking of keeping livestock on a larger scale, chickens are an excellent way to break yourself in before moving on to animals who need more care and attention.

Despite popular opinion, you don't need a lot of land to keep chickens – in fact, they will help you look after whatever land you do have. They love eating insects, slugs, weeds and grass clippings, and will supply you with quality compost. If you do happen to have a fair bit of space, you can move the chickens around every few months so that the land doesn't become boggy in one patch. Next year, I plan to get a big shed on runners like skis – it may sound bonkers but then I can pull my chickens around the farm to different

ABOVE Foxes aren't a problem on the farm, so the chickens can roam around to their hearts' content.

spots to keep turning over the land. It just makes sense. But keep an eye on where you put them – chickens don't discriminate. I let them loose and they ended up digging for worms in Michaela's flower garden. They wrecked all her plants and I was in the doghouse for a good few days.

When we first brought our chickens to the farm, we enclosed them for a couple of weeks to get them used to their hut and prevent them from wandering off or disappearing. After that, they seemed to know where they lived and always returned home, so we were able to let them roam. When the chickens first arrived, we kept quietly creeping into their hut to check for eggs, then slowly creeping out again empty-handed. After a few weeks of this, we finally discovered our first egg – it was a wonderful moment and so exciting to get the first produce from our own animals. I fried it as part of a hearty breakfast and it tasted terrific. After that, our hens seemed to settle and would lay eight or nine eggs every day, which was brilliant. I've never eaten so many delicious eggs. Then a few months later, just as we were doing well, the chickens suddenly stopped laying altogether. This left us all scratching our heads, wondering what we'd done wrong. Eventually we found out that there was no great mystery to the go-slow chickens – they had just gone into moult and didn't want to lay for a while.

To my mind, there's nothing like chickens for making a farm feel like the real thing. I was happy to have plenty of them and let my flock increase naturally. Soon we had a fairly even mix of cockerels and hens: the idea is to let the hens lay and to eat the cocks but the

Tips on Keeping Chickens

● You can keep free-range chickens wherever you are, town or country. As long as you have a small stretch of land and enough room for a pen, you have enough room to give them a happy existence; but if you live in a built-up area, you should check with your neighbours about the noise before buying, especially if you want a cockerel. You should also check with the local authorities as some impose restrictions on keeping livestock.

● Start off small with a trio of, say, two hens and a cockerel; you can aim to increase the size of your flock as time goes by. If you want to increase the number of chickens you have and like the sight of chicks hopping around, then it's a good idea to let the process happen organically. All the eggs that are laid will be fertile. It may sound obvious, but you should bear in mind that you never know what sex you'll get when your eggs hatch.

● If you buy chickens when they are very young, they need a lot of care. A good option for novices is to buy your hens at point of lay, in other words, young females on the point of laying their first eggs, usually when they are around eight months old. Point-of-lay chickens will be advertised as such, and they will reward you almost immediately with eggs. This will instantly give you confidence in your farming abilities – finding your first egg is an experience you won't forget, believe me.

● You don't need to invest hundreds of pounds in fencing or ready-made huts; you can make a pen out of anything you have lying around, if you aren't too worried about the look of a slap-dash ramshackle at the end of your garden. Utilise bits of tin, planks of wood, and old crates for nesting boxes. Use your imagination. If that all sounds too much like hard work, then you can easily convert a garden shed or buy a cheap one from your local DIY store for less

than £100 (you'll probably save that much cash not having to buy eggs for a year). This may work out cheaper than a ready-made ark, which is a well-designed hut especially for chickens that comes in a variety of sizes.

● A chicken hut should be clean, dry and well ventilated without being draughty. Hens don't seem to mind the cold, but they hate damp, windy conditions. Also essential is a perch for roosting and a nest box below for the hens to lay their eggs in. If you are making your own chicken hut, or adapting a garden shed, I would recommend that you use a piece of dowel that is 2 inches thick or a large broom handle to construct your perch. This is about the right size for them to grip. Using something too wide or too narrow will mean that your chickens will just keep falling off it or, worse, develop physical ailments trying to do what doesn't come naturally. You also need to make sure that the perch is the highest element in the chicken house, because if it isn't, the birds will try and use whatever is. I would also recommend putting a piece of hardboard under your perch to catch droppings. If it is a size that you can manoeuvre in and out of the chicken house each morning, you can scrape it straight into your compost heap. This will keep the hut clean (not to mention you) and your compost thriving in one hit.

● You can make a nest box from an old crate or cardboard box, but do remember to make it draught-proof and cosy with some clean straw. Hens, like any other birds, love making nests. Make sure that you can reach the nesting boxes easily – you'll find that sometimes your hens will be reluctant to move off an egg, despite you calling them all sorts of names as they nip you.

● Remember to ensure that your shelter is safe from predators: foxes, cats, dogs, badgers, in fact, just about anything will eat them. Your flock also needs easy access to the outdoors. Make sure the door on the hut opens and closes smoothly and is simple for the birds to get in and out of. I recommend letting your chickens have free roam of your land or their pen during the day and putting them inside safely each night, away from predators.

● Feeding chickens is easy. You'll find that any of the traditional breeds are pretty happy foraging for most of their diet in the summer months. We hardly feed our chickens at all between June and October. There were thousands of grasshoppers and crickets around for them to munch, giving them a real high-protein diet, which we bolstered with kitchen scraps and peelings for extra vitamins and minerals. In winter and spring-time, when there is less grass and fewer grubs and roots for them to find, your birds will rely on you for food. Their staple diet should be maize, corn and rolled barley. You can give this grain to your birds in abundance and, unlike pigs, they will eat only what they need. Replenish their lack of greens with the outer leaves of any leafy vegetables from your kitchen or garden, which will provide them with plenty of calcium and supplement the grain diet. The golden rule is to remember that the quality of your feed will be reflected in your eggs and meat. So will flavour, so avoid giving your chickens scraps with strong flavours, such as garlic, fish or curry, which may not only give you a strange-tasting breakfast experience, but will undoubtedly upset their stomachs too. If you want lovely fresh eggs and meat, feed your chickens lovely fresh food. You'll all be happy.

little blighters are very nippy on their feet and we never seem to catch them – they're all over the place. I don't mind too much because I think cockerels look splendid. It's true that they do wake you up at the crack of dawn and most of them sound great, but not everyone appreciates the pleasures of such an early morning call. I've got about fifteen cockerels that sit outside my window every morning – some of them sound truly magnificent but you have to be prepared to get a few that can't quite manage a 'cock-a-doodle-do' and loudly croak and screech out of tune instead.

Keeping chickens isn't difficult, especially if they are free range, and it's amazing what a difference a free-range lifestyle makes to a chicken. The Black Rocks are usually fairly docile and have a strong immunity but my lot had always been kept indoors when I bought them. The once-handsome chooks had turned into scrawny, scraggy fowl who were nervous of the big outside world. A few weeks after Rick and I had introduced them to life in the great outdoors, they were like new birds. Their glossy black feathers gave a healthy green gleam when the sun hit their backs, their chests and bellies broadened and they proudly sported the now-tufty chestnut feathers around their necks as they strutted their stuff around the farm. Not only do free-range fowl make for happy pets but, as you probably already know from buying and eating free-range eggs and meat, your tastebuds will be rewarded for giving your chickens a healthy life.

Light my fire

This summer, just like our chickens, we ended up spending most of our time outdoors. We worked and socialised out in the open, enjoying great weather and company as well as hard graft. As the dry dusty days with their big skies gave way to balmy evenings, we'd sit around on straw bales, drinking beer and chatting, feeling the satisfaction of a few mild aches from physical work and that stretchy feeling your face has when it's been in the sun all day. We'd often be in the company of friends, who would travel up to the farm from London for the weekend to soak up a bit of the good life. They loved to escape their city lives and, to our surprise, after a busy week at work were often keen to help out on the farm too. Inspired by their enthusiasm, the good old country tradition of calling in and returning favours, and the desperate need to push work along on the farm, we decided to hold a working party. What better way to work than with your mates, offering them a Cowboys-and-Indians-themed barbecue and disco in return for their efforts?

The day of the working party had to be one of the hottest of the year. I opened the door of the mobile home that morning to be greeted with a muggy heat of sauna intensity and swarms of flies as I traipsed across the farm to let out the chickens. And it was only 7.30am. Michaela was already up, making lists of the jobs we needed to tackle, with her breakfast in one hand, a pen in the other. Just a couple of hours later, as we were getting into our daily duties, we heard the sound of wheels on gravel – our workers had begun to

OPPOSITE Some of our working party volunteers removing decades of dirt and decay from the loose boxes so that we could turn them into warm winter lodgings for the pigs.

arrive. About fifty people showed up in total, smothered in sunblock, wearing vest tops and jeans, ready for action. It was a fantastic turn-out. Michaela insisted that I organise the rowdy rabble into groups and refer to her list as a reminder, not entirely trusting my claim that it was all in my head. So some scooted off to clear out the barn while others tidied up the loose boxes. A group of guys chopped down some dead trees, and women cleared the bracken in the orchard, ready for seeds to be sown. Another group painted the house, someone strimmed the grass, and Michaela's mates dug up the stinging nettles, weeds and rotten vegetation in the garden she had started to create. I remember stopping work at one stage, to grab a swig of water; I looked around and the farm was alive with people, all chipping in, laughing, getting a tan and working really hard, their figures obscured by the heat haze in front of me. It was an amazing feeling.

By the afternoon, we had generated a huge heap of dead wood and debris, so I set my cousins Amy, Beth and Fay the task of burning it. They lit a small fire and added the wood and rubbish to the smouldering stack bit by bit. But this was not a normal fire – the land was so dry and the field had been derelict for so long that the grass had grown and died in layers, which made the fire burn intensely. We all became nervous as the wind picked up, throwing the direction of the flames to the west and all too quickly, a spark hit a patch of the dry grass, setting it alight. The fire started to spread swiftly as twenty of us ran to fetch buckets of water and sand to try and douse it. Despite our very best efforts, it swiftly torched the whole field. We shouted the rest of the workers over to help but, although all hands were on deck and armed with buckets, we couldn't keep up with the flames. Then the wind changed direction and took the fire on a different course. It jumped the back fence and headed for the field that ran down to the railway track. We chased it in vain.

This was frightening – the fire was out of control and a danger to farm and everything and everyone on it. Just when we thought we had it under control, it would spring up somewhere else, roaring off at the most incredible speed. We knew we couldn't handle this alone and soon the fire brigade were coming up, sirens blaring and hoses at the ready. The fire had started to cause chaos beyond the farm as it raged away. The railway track was closed, along with a section of the A14, and the army phoned to say they had eighteen Green Goddesses on standby and helicopters circling the area. No one in Ipswich could open their windows on that steamy summer afternoon, because of the smoke. The fire brigade used up all the water on the farm trying to rein in the fire and had to go back to headquarters for more supplies as there was nothing nearby, but, towards evening, the fire was finally brought under control and put out.

There was a huge dip in morale on the farm as everyone stood around, astonished at what had happened and the devastation it seemed to cause. We had all been badly shaken up but once the danger was over and I realised with relief that no serious damage had been done and no one had been hurt, I decided we needed a big drink to get back on track. So I made all fifty people line up for a bottle of beer and a laugh before cracking on with their tasks. The only good thing to come out of the unfortunate fire was that we invited all the firemen to the party that evening, which seemed to make the girls very happy indeed!

And what a night. Perhaps part of it was relief, and a release from the tension that the fire had caused, but we had a fantastic time. We had made a huge chilli and prepared a barbecue designed to quash the biggest appetites in reward for such sterling work. Even Peter Gott paid us a visit, bringing us some of his superb home-made sausages. Underneath an amazing electric storm we danced, dressed as cowboys and Indians, pausing only to marvel at the forks of lightning and rumbles of thunder, wondering if the rain we could have done with earlier would now come. But it never did.

The next morning, I awoke excited, keen to see just what we had achieved the previous day. After feeding the chickens, Michaela and I took a stroll around the farm, clearing up from the party with slightly sore heads and the sun beating down on our necks. Although the fire had been a disaster, disrupting the whole of Ipswich and scarring the land, the working party had been a great success. Everybody's huge efforts had paid off with obvious results. The outside of the farmhouse looked great thanks to a coat of

BELOW The fire that took place in our first summer took hours to get under control, but thanks to the sterling effort of the fire brigade, all was well in the end.

paint, although it remained derelict inside; the garden was clear of debris; the dead trees had gone and the orchard had been cleared, as had the barn and all the loose boxes. It felt and looked as though we had made real headway. It looked a different place to the one I had arrived at with Asa and Rick four months before. Twenty years of rubbish had been cleared away, the fencing put up, walls constructed and buildings mended. It looked, at last, like a farm that meant business.

The long hot summer days never seemed to end and they reminded me of being a boy, playing in the woodland during my school holidays, building makeshift aviaries and watching my ferrets play. I remember using every free moment to explore nature and I loved it. The difference now was that we were immersing ourselves in some serious physical graft but a precious hour grabbed here and there to relax and enjoy the countryside, the wildlife and all we had set up so far, made Rick, Michaela and me feel as though we were really living the dream. So when the mood took me and I needed a break from the farm, off I would go, scouring the neighbouring countryside in search of whatever I could find in the way of really tasty wild treats to take home to Michaela for our supper.

BELOW The party we had following the fire was fantastic. Fuelled by relief, huge quantities of beer and mountains of food, it was a terrific way to unwind after a gruelling day.

Fresh and wild

Before you baulk at the idea of foraging in hedgerows for food and put it down as something I must have picked up as a survival tactic in the TA, I've got to tell you that finding your own wild produce is far more rewarding than any shopping experience. You just need to know where to look and find what is seasonally stored in nature's pantry to claim it as yours – as long as you're not straying on to private land, of course. It's completely natural, it's free and you have the satisfaction of knowing that you have hand-plucked the little gems you've discovered in the soil. You can find all manner of edible fruit, vegetables, shoots, flowers and herbs if you just open your eyes, and these treasures don't always pop up in secluded leafy spots in the depths of the countryside either – I have to confess that, having seen the price of rosemary in a well-known supermarket in Coventry, I left it on the shelf, only to find exactly what the store was charging £2.00 a sprig for growing naturally on a public footpath opposite! Another herb you'll find growing wild at this time of year is mint, which is great for adding a fresh zing to your salads and potatoes, and for making a simple but delicious fresh-mint teat. Just add hot water and sugar or honey.

That's not all. This summer I found wild samphire in the marshes as well as elderflowers, and later elderberries, in the woods. Samphire is a coastal plant that is a bit like asparagus and tastes just as good. The Romans used to eat it and it now commands a premium in farmers' markets, so it's well worth looking out for in the summer months, especially if you live by the sea. Take the tender shoots from the plant, leaving the roots in the ground. Then treat the shoots as you would asparagus: steamed or simmered until al dente and served with a big knob of English butter. Fantastic.

As for elderflowers, they are everywhere in the countryside at the beginning of summer, including woody areas and on roadsides, when their heady scent and delicate white flowers pop up in abundance. The flowers are particularly good for making cordial – see my recipe on page 214. Towards the end of August, you'll find elderberries in their wake. Despite popular opinion, the berries aren't poisonous – in fact they are positively delicious, adding a wonderful tart flavour to salads and ice creams, but remember to balance the sharpness with a little more sugar than usual.

If foraging in the hedgerows is just not your style, then there are other ways of getting your hands on produce that is far fresher and more delicious than what's on offer at your local supermarket. Farmers' markets seem to be making a strong and very welcome presence in the UK. They have popped up all over the country during the last couple of years, offering a vast selection of seasonal vegetables and fruit, breads, cheeses, fish and meat each week, at a public space near you; see my list at the back of the book for some of the best around. If you visit, you'll find vegetables and fruit that are brightly coloured, firm to the touch and ooze that just-plucked-from-the-field freshness. Most will be organic but, more importantly, the majority will be seasonally and locally grown and that is the key. Seasonal produce will have been very recently picked rather than stored for months or air-freighted in from a foreign country, which depletes vital nutrients and means that by the time it reaches our table, it makes for a lifeless, watery offering. The fresh stuff will also be reasonably priced – of course, this price may work out at a few pence more per kilo for farm quality above what the supermarket can offer you; supermarkets can negotiate an unrealistically low price, having bought their produce from a supplier in bulk. Whenever major food retailers offer extremely low prices, someone is losing out – and you can bet it isn't the supermarket. So I suggest you turn your shopping list on its head and think of quality as defining your purchases, rather than quantity for comparable cash, and you'll still end up with value for money. You can't lose. What's more, buying your produce at a market is a relaxing and enjoyable experience. I often end up chatting to the stall holders while looking at the lovely things on offer and even picking up a few samples to taste as I wander around. As you can probably tell, I'm a great fan of markets and I'm sure that, if you haven't already, once you've tried it, you'll be hooked as well.

Growing your own

The best way to get hold of fresh, cheap vegetables is to grow your own produce. It's an excellent idea and one I was keen to try during our first summer on the farm. Eager to embark on the dream of eating what I grew, I couldn't wait to get cracking even though summer isn't the best time to begin planting. I would recommend starting in autumn or spring if you want the best results. Then, come summer, you'll be rewarded with splendid harvests. Summer is the most productive season in established kitchen and fruit gardens, and, with a little perseverance, you'll get a fine crop of home-grown soft fruits and berries, peas, beans (runners and French), lettuces, cucumbers, and, by late summer, shallots and tomatoes, most of which will need picking daily. You'll be overwhelmed with your bounty and may even want to try the traditional preserving methods of bottling, pickling and jam-making. Or there's always the good old freezer . . . But this year, I was just at the beginning.

To start my vegetable patch, I decided to set aside a corner of the farm that was slightly tucked out of the way, but any strip of land will do. If space is really tight, you can always grow herbs in window boxes or on sills.

It's rare that you'll be blessed with the perfect conditions for growing vegetables in your garden, so as long as you've picked a spot that is flat and enjoys sun as well as shade, don't waste time fretting. It's much more productive to work with what you've already got. With this in mind, the first thing I did on my vegetable patch was to test the

OPPOSITE **Whenever time allows, there's nothing I like better than wandering round the countryside, particularly when it's my own farm.**

soil – you can pick up a kit at the garden centre to do this. Ideally, the pH levels should be neutral at seven on the scale of zero to fourteen, but there is no need to abandon your project if they're not. If the land is too acidic (i.e. below seven), you can buy organic agents to bring the level down, and if it is too alkaline, you can add some well-rotted manure to bring up the acidity. And don't despair if you find that spot of land you want to start your veg patch on is clay. Try adding a layer of well-rotted compost or free-draining grit before adding another layer of manure or top soil. First things first, though – before you add anything to your soil, get rid of any weeds.

We were unlucky enough to have Japanese knotweed absolutely everywhere this summer; it's a real pest and it's very persistent. Despite Asa's attempts to chop it back, I don't think we'll ever be able to banish it completely without using a ton of pretty nasty chemicals, which is not something I'd consider. The best thing to do is wage war on weeds with your hoe in the summer months. At this time of year the weeds run rampant and take over if you don't keep digging the little rascals up at the roots. It's really hard work but it has to be done.

In text books and serious gardening manuals there are a load of hard and fast rules about how to grow vegetables. In my opinion it's best to ignore the majority of them and experiment for yourself – it's much more fun, and you'll learn more by trial and error, so go for it! People have said that my vegetable patches look chaotic but there is some method to what these people see as madness. If you harvest all of your crop on a particular week of the season, as some of these books suggest, then you'll end up with a ton of one vegetable at its peak and you won't know what to do with it all. I'm not averse to harvesting a little early when you just can't wait to sample the joy of a few tender leaves, and then look forward to a second crop. The big no-no in these books is letting things go to seed – but, every now and then, if your larder is full, why not let your veggies go over? Leave them alone and see what happens if you let nature follow its course. Some sprout amazing flowers or shoots; they're not good to eat but they can look the business.

If you do start your patch in summer, the beginning of the season is the best time to plant tender crops like tomatoes. And this year, Rick had his own tomato mission. He'd grown a tomato plant in a pot and wanted to set it free. Unfortunately, despite some serious TLC, the plant didn't like the conversion from pot to soil and didn't make it past a few weeks. Despite this initial setback, I still plan to grow tomatoes next year and I'm keen to do it from the seeds of the fruit itself. You can grow tomatoes successfully this way if you scoop out the seeds from the flesh of the tomato and dry them out on some kitchen paper before dropping them carefully into the ground. This way you can even wait until you find a tomato you really like the taste of before growing a crop of them. But this seemed a bit adventurous for the beginning of our patch, so I tried my luck with cabbages and lettuces, easy vegetables to start experimenting with.

OPPOSITE A farm wouldn't be a proper farm without some crops, so I decided to cultivate a small plot of land to supply fresh veg for the table.

ABOVE Sow seeds in trays, or buy them ready germinated, and keep somewhere warm until the seedlings are large enough to plant outside. You'll soon be rewarded with your very own crop of fresh veg.

You can't really go wrong planting cabbages and lettuces as long as your soil is well drained. You can buy the plants as seedlings, already germinated, and then simply fit the leafy crops into your plot, leaving enough growing space around each. Simple. Don't feel confined to growing English varieties of lettuce either; you can buy trays of mixed foreign lettuces as well as choosing your favourite home-grown varieties. I'm particularly keen on a couple of Italian varieties, lollo rosso and rocket. The beauty of lollo rosso is that you needn't harvest the whole plant in one go, just pick a few leaves as you fancy eating them. And if you throw some rocket seeds down in your patch and wait for that to shoot up, you can pick a handful to have with your lollo rosso too. You'll never want to buy a bag of wet, mushy leaves from the supermarket again! Or you could consider it one last time and invest in a bag of watercress to grow indoors. Kids in particular love this. All you need to do is fill a very large glass dish or an aquarium with water, pour in some gravel, plant the watercress in the gravel, it will quickly root. Keep the container on a window ledge. Harvest the leaves that sit above the water and this will give you never-ending salad and great value from one bag. Remember to change the water regularly.

Our first crop of home-grown lettuces were fantastic this year, thanks to the glorious weather and some natural yet vigilant pest control. It seemed as though our cabbages and lettuces were as popular with slugs and other insects as they were with us. To deter white cabbage butterflies, we planted alliums like garlic, onions and chives in between our crops. The pungent smell masks that of the cabbage, and tricks any swooping demons into shooting off in search of another patch. As for slugs, we found that sprinkling salt and chilli powder on the soil between the crops was an extremely effective deterrent, until it rained; then we put out the skins of grapefruit halves after we'd eaten the pulp, or crushed eggshells, depending on what we'd had for breakfast. They absolutely hate both of these things.

The key to successful pest control is to live with them rather than start a losing battle by spraying the bugs – and inevitably your plants – with nasty chemicals. Although, if all else fails, you may catch yourself hovering over your vegetable patch with a torch in the night, trying to catch slugs. If you have the luxury of room in your garden, one of the most effective ways of keeping your bug count low is to build a pond. If you include a log pile in the design, it will enable your predators (namely frogs, toads and ground beetles) to sneak out at night and catch the pests for you. There are good insects and bad – the good ones help along your vegetables by killing the pests who love to consume the tasty produce. This is another reason not to get out the sprays – you can often kill off the good insects as well as the bad, which does no good at all and totally disrupts the natural order of things.

In the summer, any salad crops you have previously sown will reach their best, but I would recommend that you carry on planting lettuces, radishes and spring onions every few weeks to give you a constant supply of tasty salads throughout the summer months. At the end of July or the beginning of August you can also sow your salads for autumn and winter (endives and chicory, for example). And, if you've already planted them, your early potatoes will be ready to pick, but keep your eyes on the main crop, especially in August, when they can get struck by blight.

Potatoes are a wonderful crop to grow – I don't have to tell you all the uses they can be put to. They've had a bad press recently with all these diets that are doing the rounds, but don't listen because they're an excellent source of protein, fibre, minerals and vitamins, particularly vitamin C. So follow my tips below for a bumper crop of spuds. . .

Are you tempted yet? Even if you have limited space, you don't need to limit your horizons. A small walled city garden can be a great home to a fanned apple or even a peach tree. Plant it against a wall to give yourself maximum space as well as fruit that's been ripened from the heat of the wall. Peas are dead easy and will grow up the wall in a similar way. I've even grown carrots in an old chimney stack (the only time you get short carrots is if your vegetable bed isn't big enough). Don't feel left out if you haven't got a garden – you can grow a small crop of chillis or tomatoes in a window box. Just try it. I bet the tomatoes you pick from your own ledge will be the best tomatoes you've ever tasted and a real talking point if you're sharing a meal with friends.

Herbs are also great to grow in flower or window boxes. All you need is a deep pot and then you can plant thyme, rosemary, parsley or any of the Mediterranean herbs like

Tips on Growing Potatoes

● Potatoes grow best in deep, well-drained soil of pretty much any type, though a neutral or slightly acidic soil works best. Try and find a sunny spot that's not too exposed or liable to frost. If you're planning well in advance, prepare your soil the previous autumn with lots of well-rotted manure or compost dug through the earth. If not, don't worry. Just prepare your ground in the spring before planting.

● The simplest way to start is to buy seed potatoes and plant them in rows. If you want to be extra-clever, you can do something called 'chitting', which is simply bringing on the sprouting before planting. Stand the seed potatoes in trays in lots of light and wait for the shoots to reach about an inch long – it should take about six weeks so get going in late January or early February for spring planting. Don't use the sprouters that have been sitting in your vegetable rack for too long, as they can create virus problems.

● Dig trenches 9 inches deep and 2 feet apart for your seed potatoes and plant when the heavy frosts are over. Carefully placed the sprouting seedlings on a light layer of fertiliser, with the sprouts facing upwards, about a foot apart. As soon as the shoots appear, cover each row with a ridge of soil so that the shoots are just buried. Keep doing this as the shoots break free – by the time the potatoes are ready, the ridge will be about 6 inches high.

This process helps to protect the shoots from frost and blight and reduces the number of green potatoes – they need to grow in the dark or they won't be fit for eating. This regular soil work will also keep the weeds in check. Remember to water regularly if there isn't enough rain.

● Potatoes should be ready for lifting from June to September depending on the variety. Cut off the tops two weeks before you lift to toughen the potato skins. If you think you might have blight, cut off the tops, wait two weeks and then lift. The blight doesn't travel through the plant, it is usually washed down on to the potatoes by rain. Try and lift your crop on a nice sunny day – it will come out easily and you can let the potatoes dry for a little before you bag them. But remember – too much sunlight turns them green and green potatoes are poisonous. Don't feed them, or the plant leaves, to livestock – they are full of prussic acid.

● You can also grow potatoes in containers, if your space is limited. You'll need a container that is deep, and well drained: half fill it with compost or garden soil, put two seed potatoes on top and then cover with more compost or soil to within about an inch of the container rim. Keep it well watered and follow the instructions in paragraph 3.

basil or oregano, all of which will do well in the summer months. If this is all new to you, you'll be looking for some instant gratification from your plants, so I would suggest that you buy your herbs from a nursery. Let someone else do the hard work from seeds or cuttings and maybe think of trying this when you have more experience as well as time. I wouldn't recommend that you buy your growing herbs from the supermarket, however, as their often bright-green appearance is an indication that they have been forced prematurely under lights. Pay a bit more for something that is better quality and English grown. Just remember to water your herbs, give them plenty of natural light and pick their leaves regularly. This will mean you'll have an abundance of healthy herbs to add delicious flavours to your cooking and your plants will stay healthy as they shoot up again, responding to being cut back. These things are vital for happy herbs.

If you are planning to plant herbs in the garden, you can have even more fun. Many herbs will look after themselves, if you follow the rules above and pop them into well-cultivated soil. The Mediterranean varieties such as sage and basil like it dry and hot, so if next summer is anything like this one, you should be fine. If you have time beyond this, you can be a little bit more creative. Why not germinate your herbs from seed, using a lemonade bottle cut in half to create an instant miniature greenhouse? You could also choose to grow some variegated herbs, where the leaves have a pretty two-colour effect, as not all of your herbs need to be solely for eating. They will look fantastic as plants in your garden and are very attractive, especially varieties such as lemon thyme and apple mint. Chocolate mint is a great one to grow too, it looks and tastes sensational rolled up and plopped into a long cool gin and tonic with some ice. Talking of mint of the more regular variety, beware – constrict its growth by planting in a pot or container or it will take over your garden. It grows rampantly and very, very fast. Your herbs will come to an end as the summer days make way for chillier mornings and evenings. But you needn't be without a fresh supply for your cooking. Move your potted plants inside to a kitchen window, or harvest your whole crop and freeze it, allowing you to add your herbs to your saucepan throughout the winter.

It wasn't just our vegetable patch and herb garden that kicked off to a promising start this summer. The odd shoot of grass began to pop up on the patch of land around the caravans as Michaela persevered with her plan to transform the area into a country garden. She was keen for the farm to be somewhere nice for us all to live and she knew that we would be trundling home through a muddy bog by the autumn if we didn't do something about it now. At the weekends, she would come up from London to help out on the farm, always making time to visit the garden centre to buy grass seed and plants. She sowed the seeds and planted roses and clematis along the red-brick wall, so that the flowers would soften the visual impact of the mobile homes. In the blazing sun, it was all very hot work; the moles and chickens became Michaela's enemies, but she had a trusty little helper to make things a little easier.

Rick would often bring his daughter Jade up to the farm at weekends. Although she was only eight years old, Jade would muck in with the rest of us, thoughtfully tidying up behind our dirty work, helping where she could and making endless cups of tea. In the long school holidays, she came up to the farm with her school friends, proudly giving them the guided tour, introducing them to the chickens and showing them her favourite spots. Jade would play on the rope swing Rick had made for her, and she would also play tricks on me. I often took a great gulp of tea she'd made, thirsty after a load of hard work, to find that she had half-filled it with salt! The little monkey soon became Michaela's chief helper in the garden. When Michaela laid grass seed, Jade stood guard against the chickens (who liked nothing more than pecking up the seed), throwing apples and shouting at them to get off the garden, without walking on it herself. She'd keep watch for hours, determined that the grass would grow. She was brilliant! And her hard work seemed to pay off. The grass did well, responding to a few warm summer showers and the blazing sunshine.

By the time the bright young blades really shot up, they seemed to mark Michaela's permanent arrival on the farm. She had moved in. Since Rick and I had set up camp in the mobile homes, Michaela had come to the farm most weekends, and she loved it. So when her most recent TV job came to an end, it seemed only natural that she move here too. After all, she was spending much more of her free time in Suffolk than in the city, despite her career in television. But the move also meant a three- or four-hour-a-day commute to work in London and the transition wasn't easy. Those long hot summer days started at 6am for Michaela, which seemed like an appalling hour for a girl who usually rolled into

BELOW The golden summer evenings were a special time that I always looked forward to sharing with Michaela after her daily journey back from the city.

ABOVE My dog Cora always accompanies me on my walks round the farm. In the early days it seemed that no matter how much work had been done, there was always masses more to do.

her TV office at 10am after a twenty-minute tube ride. At that time we had electricity and water on the farm, but no means of heating it so, just after the cockerels crowed, Michaela would be boiling kettles of water on the stove in order to fill up the shower tray, have a mini bath and wash her hair. It took about an hour to heat up enough water to perform the daily ritual, leaving her no time for breakfast before running out the door, wafting the flies away as she headed out of the dry, dusty farm for the train station. After a two hour-train journey, Michaela would find herself rudely confronted by millions of people as she came out of the station and on to one of London's busiest streets. It was a big contrast from two blokes, a few chickens and what must have seemed like a vast open space on the farm! Once when she was at her desk, she told me, she looked around the smart office and thought, 'Blimey, what's that stench?' – she looked down and had to hurry off to the loo to wash chicken poo off her shoes! It wasn't easy. But at the end of each day, she would always rush back home, in a race against the light, so that she could spend some time on the farm before the sun went down. We'd grab a glass of wine and wander around the fields and woodland, checking up on the animals before sunset, recounting the stories of our day and I'd think: 'This girl has really given up her London life to do this.' So as soon as I could arrange it, I called Michaela at work to tell her we had hot water for showers and heating for the coming winter – I have never heard her sound so excited! The advent of those little luxuries went down well with Rick, too. His family had stayed over the odd weekend and now there was talk of their moving to the farm permanently. But first came the arrival of more animals!

Ducks 'n' geese

My dream farm had always been the sort you see in storybooks, with all kinds of animals on it – in other words, a mixed livestock farm. Although the pigs were going to be the mainstay of the business, I reckoned that more poultry would help the character of the place and offer us a greater variety of produce to sell in the farm shop, which could only be a good thing. We had chickens, of course, but now I was keen to try my hand at other kinds of fowl as well. One steamy summer afternoon, I decided to take a trip to Cambridge. The windows were rolled down on the truck, the sleeves of my t-shirt flapped in the wind, but my shades still stuck to my face with the heat. I was off to see a man about some ducks and geese. After a quick look around Mark Burton's farm and his 800-strong army of free-range poultry, we struck a deal and I swiftly drove back to the farm with ten birds carefully cooped up in the truck. It may not sound like many, but Mark told me that he had started with just six or seven himself. As soon as I arrived at the farm, I was keen to get the poultry out of the truck and into my newly clean and cosy loose boxes, where the rowdy rabble stayed until they settled in. Michaela came home that night, excited to see the Indian Runner chicks, Khaki Campbell ducks and a flock of snowy-white geese that looked beautiful but were already being territorial about their new space.

In fact, the geese turned out to be the best guard dogs I've ever owned, putting Cora to shame once they were left to roam the farm. They pecked and chased everyone who visited, although this same bolshie temperament made them difficult to herd back to shelter for the evenings and I sometimes wondered who was herding who. But come the following spring, they would lay the largest eggs you've ever seen – about seven or eight times the size of a chicken egg. They were fantastic for making omelettes and had comedy value when boiled for breakfast, requiring an army of soldiers and an *Alice in Wonderland* egg cup to eat them from. Goose eggs taste amazing, but expect them only in springtime, as the birds have a very short laying period. And if you end up with a lot of ganders (male geese), then fatten them up on a natural diet and they will be a delicious addition to your dinner table at Christmas.

I would suggest you only keep geese if you have a large garden. Do so and you'll find that you'll never need to spend another Sunday morning mowing the lawn. They eat tons of grass but they also love water so you will need a wide, shallow pool where they can clean and preen themselves. Geese need to do this regularly – they are water birds and want to get their heads and necks wet, so don't be tempted to provide anything but a wide pool of good depth, or your geese will get stuck trying to immerse themselves. A large, rigid, plastic paddling pool is ideal, as long as you change the water regularly and clean it out.

BELOW Geese were among the second batch of livestock I introduced to the farm.

If you are lucky enough to have a large pond or river with a decent-sized patch of surrounding land, you also have the perfect conditions for keeping ducks. Ducks love to rummage around in the water for the odd snack as well as forage on the land surrounding it. As with chickens, you will need to supplement their natural diet for most of the year and it's important to keep their feeder in close proximity to their pond or pool, otherwise the ducks will run back and forward regularly from feeder to water and ultimately will create a very muddy path between the two. Ducks and geese don't need to roost like hens do, but they do need somewhere warm and safe to spend the night, away from predators. Basically, apart from roosting and the need for access to water, the husbandry rules are the same for all poultry, so you can refer to my section on how to feed and house chickens (see pages 32-3).

Ducks are fantastic characters and make great pets: they all seem to have their unique personalities, which really liven up our daily life on the farm. Rick brought some Kaiagoo ducks during the summer and they were so different to the sprightly Khaki Campbells and Indian Runners that had already settled in. The Kaiagoos are a North American breed, a distant relation of the Mallard, and they're big and fat. In fact, they looked ridiculous in comparison to our skinny Indian Runners. As soon as they came on to the farm, Rick put them all in the same pen as the other ducks, and in the morning, when we opened up the door, the Indian Runners went through their usual routine, standing up on their toes and shooting out of the door with the speed of Road Runner, heading for the

ABOVE Geese are very territorial animals, so they make wonderful guards, flapping and hissing at anyone who crosses their path. Unfortunately, that included me.

water before you had a chance to blink. But Rick's Kaiagoos just sat there, looking at us, moving a little, having a look around as if they were thinking, 'Huh? Where did those other ducks go?" before waddling out of the door, as if to say, 'What's the rush?' They were so slow that Rick ended up picking them up and taking them down to the water to catch up with the others.

Ducks are also great to eat, if you choose a meat breed like the Aylesbury, and lay large, rich, tasty eggs. If you opt for a laying variety like the Indian Runner, it's worth rembering that their laying periods are throughout spring and early summer. Duck eggs are much richer than chicken's, although not as rich or large as a goose's, and are excellent for baking or frying. When I was a kid I used to go down to our Mallards' nest and take, say, two eggs if the ducks had laid ten. I remember the taste of these eggs, the albumen was a brilliant shade of white and the yellow yolk stood proud and slightly convex until mopped up with a fresh piece of bread. Nothing we ever bought from the supermarket could match it for the rest of the year.

The real appeal of keeping poultry, for me, is eggs in all their wonderful varieties. Chicken, ducks and geese lay many types that vary in shape, colour, size and speckles, depending on the species. If you buy really fresh, free-range eggs, you'll find that they have a lot of variation because they haven't been subject to the same standards of sorting as supermarket eggs, where any irregular ones are discarded. But the differences are all part of the fun, and whatever form they come in – small, pointy or green – they're all little dynamites. Different varieties are a real treat; experiment with cooking, baking and frying them and you won't be disappointed.

With the advent of chickens, ducks and geese, a vegetable patch that was coming along, and a farm that was really starting to take shape, I felt as though we had made a lot of headway. Yet there was one final big push we felt we had to make before the end of the season. We focused all of our remaining energy on building the farm shop.

I had a clear vision of a clean, white space that would house a shop selling our very own bacon, sausages, black pudding, eggs, jam and chickens as well as boxes of vegetables and herbs outside and other locally produced treats. I wanted the shop to have some country character, but also contain a fully wired office at the rear of the building, which would enable us to set up, via e-mail and fax, a postal delivery service. There would need to be space for a butchery, where meat could be prepared, and a cold room for it to be stored. And, of course, space for dry storage as well as toilet facilities at the very back. But, as it stood, the original building was little more than a large rickety shack divided into two spaces. When the dairy farm had been in full swing, one side had been home to the tractors and the other, home to the bull. The roof was in an absolutely terrible state, there were even small trees growing inside and there were huge holes in the walls. It was really difficult to know where I should make a start.

OPPOSITE Jamie was very keen to collect the produce himself!

The first task was to chop down the trees that were growing inside the building and flatten out the ground in preparation for the floor to go down. After that, I knew we would need some help with the build but I managed to rope in a couple of guys Pete Gott knew to help us out with the construction work. They came down from Cumbria to lay the floor, mixing over 20 tons of gravel to make the hardcore and cement mix to pour over the levelled earth. When the floor was fully set, we tiled it and put some thought into extending the structure. We decided to use the original buildings as our guide and keep the original beams that divided the two spaces, to add some character. The guys then used a series of crisp, white, ready-made panels to connect the space together. They slotted the panels in place with silicone adhesive before adding another white box on the back of the building to house the freezer, provide extra storage and an office and toilets. This cut a neat passageway between the two spaces. After just four days we had achieved a gleaming white box that looked like something that had just landed from another universe.

Now all we had to do was to make the shop work with its surroundings. To soften the effect of the brilliant white box, we called my brother Danny in to build a brick wall on the front of the shop, using the left-over bricks we had pulled up from around the farm. When he'd finished, the shop blended in perfectly with the landscape and other outbuildings. In fact, it looked like it had been there for sixty years at least. To finish it off, we just needed to give the shop some windows. Chris Muir's brother Dave came to the rescue, paying us a visit from Devon (where Chris had taken me on a tour of likely farms all those months ago). He kindly took two days out from his conservatory business to work on the shop, using off-cuts of glass to put windows and doors into the finished building. By now, the shop was far from up and running, but it certainly started to look the business. This vital part of the project was almost ready but we still had some work to do before it could open for trade.

The sun still blazed as August approached but we knew that in a few weeks, autumn could be well on its way. And that meant one thing . . . the arrival of pigs!

At last, some pigs!

The arrival of the first Essex pigs on the farm was a day I will never forget. It felt as though we had been working up to this moment since we had started the project five months before. We had cleared the courtyard, learnt about the breeds, set up the farm shop to sell the produce they would generate and prepared the land to give them a great, free-range life. The Essex are my big passion and, although we weren't quite ready, I couldn't wait any longer. It wasn't easy to track the livestock down, but finally I found Stephen Booth, who owns some of the last thirty registered remaining Essex pigs in the country. I headed off straightaway to Stephen's farm in Cheshire to buy eight gilts (young females) and a boar from him.

The journey was an epic one. Towing a trailer on a truck really slows you down on the motorways and you end up feeling like you're driving a caravan as you hit the hills. I took a detour via Peter Gott's place for some last-minute tips and decided to stay the night. After an early start, I arrived at Stephen's mid-morning to a warm reception, and I took a few minutes to marvel at his farm before rounding up the pigs. I had a trick up my sleeve that I had learnt from Peter to help me get them into the trailer. He always says 'Empty pockets, tame men, empty stomachs, tame lions' so I asked Stephen not to feed the pigs in the evening, so that they would be hungry and tempted to follow my orange bucket full of pig feed on to the trailer. I was relieved when it worked; these are big pigs and I didn't fancy a struggle after such a long drive. To make the way home more comfortable for them, I had put some hay down to cushion the pigs from the cold metal floor of the trailer and let them settle down and sleep before I crept the truck slowly down the drive and home. The journey took five hours and I was exhausted when we finally arrived.

Back at the farm, everyone was waiting for the pigs to arrive, running outside to meet us as I drove through the farm gates and up to the courtyard. We were careful to be quiet as I opened the back of the trailer and the pigs seemed happy to wander into their

BELOW One of my pigs makes itself at home on the farm.

ABOVE Pigs have voracious appetites and always seem to be rooting around for food. Acorns are a particular favourite. When not eating, they are sociable animals and love company.

new home. Stephen had carefully selected eight Grand Duchess females – a fine variety of Essex pig and one Dictator boar for me, which was an Essex-Saddleback cross. (For a pure line I needed a Lady Dictator boar, but they were apparently, impossible to find.) But we didn't want Blaze the boar to mate with the sows quite yet, so we separated him from them and put the sows away in their own living area where they seemed to settle quite nicely. Now, none of us had handled a boar before and we were all wary of him. We thought Blaze would be a big ferocious thing and we were very cautious of touching him, just in case he lashed out.

But, on seeing him, we realised that our boar wasn't as big as we had imagined, and he was still just a young chap. We also soon realised that he was a big softie. To our relief, Blaze loved a stroke and soon started to roll over for a good rub – but there was just one problem. Blaze didn't like being on his own. He soon showed signs of being depressed when he was isolated. He started to sleep all of the time and seemed to go off his food. I went to see him and he was lying motionless on his side and just wouldn't move. I gently pulled his ear and called his name but, after five minutes, nothing. I really started to panic and was just thinking of calling the vet, when he got up and walked off! I felt a bit of an amateur. I took this plea from Blaze that he needed a bit of company seriously; after some thought, the answer seemed simple: I put a radio in his pen with him. I have to admit to laughing when the first thing that came on was *The Archers*. But it wasn't as funny as when we changed it to Classic FM for the old boy and he smashed the radio up. It became a huge running joke with everyone that he could change station with his hoof. The radio seemed to absolutely do the trick – Blaze's temper really improved and he went back to really enjoying his food.

The summer days that followed were really hot and dry, but they were also starting to get noticeably shorter. We now had pigs to feed twice a day as well as our chickens, and the farm finally really felt as though it were finally coming to life. But, as always, there was still a whole lot more work to do, a shop to get up and running, and many more pigs to give a home to. I knew that life on the farm was just beginning.

autumn the pigs arrive

The coming of autumn

The summer of 2003 seemed to last forever and it was glorious. By the first week of September, golden strands of corn still swayed in the fields, the air was balmy and the trees remained lush and green. The transition from summer to autumn felt almost seamless, except for a slight nip in the air some mornings, the long, spectacular sunsets that lit up the early evening skies and the sudden appearance in the woodland of wild foods such as chestnuts and fungi. But while the weather remained fairly constant, the change in season brought a change in mood at the farm. We didn't need the leaves to fall to remind us that time was pressing on. There was a lot to do, a lot to lose and a farm to make work, fast.

We had achieved so much during the summer months, but it just didn't seem to be enough. I only had a certain amount of money to transform the neglected land and outbuildings, and set up a business. Just getting this far had cost more than I'd expected and the farm wasn't ready to start paying for itself yet. I could see what was left rapidly disappearing. The pressure was on to get the shop open, our produce on sale, a website up and running, and some regular stalls at farmers' markets. The Essex Pig Company needed to be fully operational but we still had a long way to go: there was so much to put into place before we could make and market our own sausages and bacon, despite the determination and commitment of everyone involved. That meant that this autumn, I had to hit the ground running. We had to increase our pig herd, learn some vital skills in producing our own stuff and start selling our products, all of it as fast as possible.

Everyone had been incredible. Mates had mucked in, old pros had helped out and a core team of troops remained a steady rock. But, despite all of this, I still couldn't quite believe it when Rick announced that his family would be moving down to live in the caravan with him. It was amazing. Rick had been completely dedicated to the farm and my vision of what it could be. He spent all of his time on the farm while his family lived miles away in their terraced house in Nuneaton, visiting whenever they could. They were missing him and, what's more, they missed the farm too, so the Spriggs' made a decision to search for places in the local school for Jade and her fourteen-year-old stepbrother Carl. Before the autumn term began, the kids made the dramatic transition from the busy town of Nuneaton, Warwickshire to the quiet Suffolk countryside. They bravely packed up their old life and waved goodbye to their friends and their mum, Lynn, who stayed behind to sort out the rental of their house. She couldn't wait to join her family, despite leaving the life she knew behind. She risked everything to be involved in the project and planned to follow her family down to the farm as quickly as she could, to set up home in the tiny caravan.

The kids settled in quickly and, although they missed their mum, it was easy to see that they loved their new way of life and Rick loved having them there. Lynn visited at weekends to see the kids and help out. It made the farm feel like a real family place

OPPOSITE The woodland on the farm is a great place to wander at any time of year, but is especially picturesque in autumn, when russet-coloured leaves carpet the ground.

especially as Michaela and I still had regular visits and support from friends and family as well, so, although the pressure was mounting, it was all hands on deck to push things forward.

Our never-ending list of tasks seemed to grow and grow as we ticked off those we'd completed at the end of each day. I held on to the fact that, after just a few months of graft, the derelict farm was now bustling with livestock. The chickens, ducks, geese and pigs brought the once-desolate land to life and were testament to our summer-time efforts.

All about pigs

The Essex pigs were doing well on the farm. They seemed to love it in the courtyard and in the paddocks. We soon discovered that they were like little bulldozers; once they had cleared bramble and bracken, they turned over the grass to snout out a beetle or a worm buried beneath the soil. Farmers used to move pigs around their land, letting them plough a field, turn the stubble over and fertilise it; then the pigs would be moved on and seed sown in the nicely prepared field. The technique was called 'pannage'. We would eventually let our pigs roam the woodland for the summer and autumn months, letting them forage a wonderful diet of wild garlic, red campion, ragged robin, beech mast, acorns, chestnuts and mushrooms, all available from the forest floor like a luxurious buffet. And in return they would aerate the loose soil, turning it over and encouraging seeds within to germinate, like greedy, industrious, four-legged gardeners.

But there just weren't enough of them. If we were going to be The Essex Pig Company, then we needed more Essex pigs! I'd started out with twenty but I needed double that number for the farm to be a going concern, with thirty of those breeding sows. Finding them, however, wasn't going to be easy. As I've mentioned, the first pigs on the farm had come from Stephen Booth, one of the holders of the last group of remaining pigs registered as Essex in England. I had more chance of giving a home to a polar bear than another twenty pure-bred Essex pigs. So, why were there so few Essex pigs? And why did I want them?

Tracking down an Essex pig is a bit like hunting a dodo. But there is good reason for this – the Essex is elusive because theoretically, it became extinct in 1967! At that time the Essex pig was crossed with the Wessex to form the Saddleback (a respected rare breed today). The amalgamation was probably because there were relatively few of either pigs around and the breeds looked pretty similar, with the same lovely markings and colouring – a white band across the shoulders of an otherwise silky black body. But they were very different pigs, with very different backgrounds and from very different areas. For this reason, one farmer, John Crowshaw, refused to crossbreed his herd. In an act of animal anarchy, he registered his pigs as Saddlebacks but did not interbreed them. So today, thanks to good old John, we can identify his pigs as pure Essex and trace their bloodline back to his Essex herd, enabling the breed to live on. These pigs are rare and hard to track down, but I was sure that it couldn't be impossible. Besides, the string of coincidences that led me to discover the Essex spurred me on in my search.

When I first embarked on my hunt for the farm and was advertising for land to rent, a man named Anthony Carter spotted one of my pleas in a local newspaper and got in touch. He had land up for grabs and knew a thing or two about pigs. His family used to show and breed Essex. Anthony told me the Essex had descended from Anglo-Saxon and Norman pigs. His grandfather had won cups at the Royal Show for his pigs and now, years later, Anthony was one of the top men in the Essex Pig Society. I'd never heard of the breed but, as he started to tell me a bit about its characteristics, I immediately fell in love with the whole idea. It felt absolutely right – I was from Essex myself; I already knew that I wanted to work with rare breeds for their superior eating qualities, their self-sufficiency and natural good health; the Essex was the indigenous pig of East Anglia, where I eventually rented the farm, and it had traditionally foraged in the great forests of the region. It was perfect. These pigs were the ideal animal for the traditional, low-intensive environment that I was trying to create and I instantly imagined keeping them in the old way, allowing them to roam in our own ancient woodland. I decided that the farm should be home to Essex pigs, among other rare breeds, and that we should cultivate the Essex breed, rather than let it fade away. But taking on the task would not be simple.

Anthony Carter and the Essex Pig Society helped me track down some more Essex pigs. I decided that we had to make haste to increase the herd of pigs. We stocked up on

BELOW I erected strong fences all over the farm, in order to keep everyone where they should be – not always easy!

ABOVE One of the members of my herd newly settled on the farm.

some healthy rare-breed Saddlebacks, a handful of Essex females and bought two pigs from a local abattoir. These poor old sows were also Saddlebacks, as thin as greyhounds, their skin riddled with lice and rings through their noses (to stop them doing what comes naturally – foraging their owners' land). Most sensible farmers probably wouldn't have touched them – they certainly didn't have enough fat on them to make good meat! – but they were pregnant, about to have litters and originally from pretty good stock, so we picked them up and brought them home. We kept them apart from the main herd for a month to make sure all was well with their health. We desperately wanted to take the rings out of their noses but they were too old not to cause complete distress to the pigs' sensitive snouts if we tried to dislodge them.

As we gave the new sows a taste of the good life, I began to think that finding and breeding pure Essex pigs rather than a near bloodline would remain a distant dream. Then, on one of those autumn days that still felt like summer, I got a phone call from a lady called Debbie, who worked in Harlow at an open farm for children to visit. She had seen an article on me in the *Anglian Times* and wondered if I'd be interested in the pigs they had on their farm. It turned out that Pet's Corner was home to all sorts of lovely rare breeds – Gloucester Old Spots, Saddleback Crosses, and pure-bred Essex pigs. I couldn't believe my ears when Debbie mentioned that they had a Lady Dictator boar too! So she asked her boss Justin Hopwood to fax me the pedigree of the boar and the pigs and, in a mix of excitement and panic, I frantically passed the information on to Stephen Booth who contacted Vaughan

Byrne, Mr Pig himself. Vaughan verified the bloodlines as being pure and extremely rare, so I quickly rang Debbie back to save the pigs' bacon – literally. They were scheduled to meet their maker. I couldn't afford to buy the boar himself, much as I would have liked to. Once the owners of the pigs realised what rare creatures they had they kindly offered me the services of the male to help increase my herd. It was much easier and cheaper to buy the services of the boar, and I was delighted to have use of his services! These important animals came frighteningly close to becoming some of those non-descript supermarket sausages! In a few months I would have more pure Essex piglets, with, I hoped, a Lady Dictator among them, and I'd be able to play my part in rescuing this wonderful rare breed from complete extinction.

As for sausages, I still didn't know how to make my own. The one thing that I did know is that the meat from rare breeds is the best for the job – the pork and bacon produced by each breed varies in texture and flavour, in very much the same way that apples do, but all are of the highest quality. The full-flavoured pork produced by a Tamworth bears as little resemblance to the delicate, light flavour of the Berkshire as a crisp Pink Lady apple does to a more earthy Russet. It's this diversity in the eating qualities of the pigs, as well as the animals themselves, that made me keen to keep a variety of rare breeds and cultivate the bloodlines that go as far back as the Iron Age. I loved the idea of offering people a variety of sausages, with recipes made from pork originating from different breeds. And, what's more, once everything was up and running, customers would be able to see the different types of pigs roaming round the farm as they visited our farm shop.

While I searched for more rare-breed pigs to give a good home to on the farm, this question of making our own sausages became more and more pressing. Some of you might find this fact of farming life hard to swallow and would not be able to turn your curly-tailed friend into a tasty joint of pork, but for me, this is business. The animal's welfare is always paramount and I am determined that my pigs will have a fantastic life but, as they reach their premium weight or have served their use as breeders, they will inevitably go to slaughter. It is essential that we stagger the animals so that, as some go to slaughter, others are about to give birth, keeping our livestock numbers high and the supply of meat dependable and regular. This cycle of life and death needed to be smoothly underway if we were going to be successful. The Essex Pig Company had to start producing meat products to sell at farmers' markets and one of the largest, most prestigious ones of all was about to take place in Covent Garden, London. Henrietta Green's Food Lovers' Fair was just weeks away and we had to be there.

A trader cannot simply pitch up to this event and set up a stall, especially a newcomer like me, without a track record or any products to sell. It's pretty exclusive and permission to trade has to be granted. So thank heavens for my mate Peter Gott! He

Tips on Keeping Pigs

• Pigs are wonderful animals to keep and they will reward you hugely. The Irish used to refer to the pig as 'the gentleman who pays the rent' because one pig could supply so much in the way of meat and saleable products. And, of course, they munch up an incredible amount of household rubbish which is the most environmentally friendly way of disposing of it. Your pig will provide with wonderful meat and the best compost – not bad.

• Start off small with one or two pigs until you get more experience. I would not recommend you get a boar first off – the best thing to do is get gilts, and have them mated when you want to breed some piglets.

• You will need some room to keep pigs, as they like to roam around. Although they spend most of their day outside they need some housing, even in the warmer months. It's easy to cobble something together from whatever you have lying around, if you don't mind a rustic look. The pigs' housing just has to be warm, dry, clean and very strong – filling the interior with straw is ideal as this provides extremely snug bedding that all the pigs can nest in.

• Pigs need water troughs for access clean, fresh water, especially sows, who drink gallons when they're pregnant. Troughs need to be very heavy or attached to the ground so that the pigs don't knock them over and low enough for the

tiniest piglets to get their share. You can either use a trough in a similar way for food, or throw down your pig feed in the fields from a bucket. I use a pig feed brand, Pig Nuts, to supply the mainstay of their diet. You can supplement this diet for your pigs with left-over kitchen scraps like vegetable peelings, greens or root vegetables that are just a little too old to eat yourself, or any left-over cold porridge – they love anything like that mixed alongside their regular feed. If you feed them potatoes, make sure they are cooked. This gives them the nutrients they need and will cut down half of what you throw away each week. In the summer months, if you are able to keep your pigs on a grassy field, they will get almost half of their sustenance from the grass, so you could do without your Pig Nuts at that time if you

continue with scraps. But remember, pigs are vegetarians, so don't feed them meat or fish from the kitchen.

• When a sow is about to farrow (give birth) you should pay extra attention to her diet until after her piglets are weaned, as she will require extra protein throughout that time. I recommend that three days before she is due, add a mixture of bran soaked in hot water that you've allowed to cool to her usual food. Continue giving her this until the piglets are weaned, after which you can reduce the amount and return to her usual food.

• Don't worry about being a novice when your sow is in pig – pregnant – as she will pretty much organise things, though she will need some space all to herself, enough room so that she can turn in comfort. When the piglets are born, there is not much that you need to do – the sow and her young are pretty self-sufficient. You may want to see that the piglets feed in the first hour. Check that they are all sucking and that a little runt isn't being bullied out of the way. It's pretty amazing, but they all seem to find their own particular teat and always return to it. The sow will take care of everything else, including bossing them around and teaching them a thing or two. When the piglets are three days old, they will be ready to see the outside world, accompanied by the sow, but avoid letting them roam outside their pen if the weather is wet. Once outside, the piglets will soon show their first signs of foraging by having munch on some grass and, at around three weeks old, they'll be ready for solid food.

kindly introduced me to Henrietta Green who knew of him, his incredible work and quality products. His recommendation was priceless but the high standard of our produce was what really counted – now all we had to do was to whip up some sample sausages for Henrietta to taste to secure our place at the big event. Sounds simple. But the farm shop was far from finished and we didn't yet have the facilities to prepare any sausages. There just wasn't enough time to complete the processing unit in the shop and get it passed by the Health Authority, as well as design and manufacture packaging for the products, all in a matter of weeks. Nevertheless I was determined that I wasn't about to miss out on the opportunity of the Fair, so I called in yet another favour from Peter and he came to my rescue. Off I went to his farm in Cumbria to learn how to make sausages – fast!

Peter Gott is a mountain of a man and, as you may have gathered, he's extremely kind of heart. If you're a friend of his, he will help you out of any situation and always smiles while he's doing it, however tough the going gets. When I have a party, Peter will often just turn up with some of his fantastic meat, throw a barbecue for my mates and kip in the barn. And he's always there to help in a crisis. But I have to be on my toes – Peter was once involved in a huge debate with DEFRA (the Department for the Environment, Food and Rural Affairs), where he was to ask why he wasn't able to produce Parma ham in the traditional way in this country, as in the rest of Europe. But when the big day of his presentation came, he'd double-booked and was going on holiday. So he faxed a load of bullet points over to me at the farm and I found myself being packed off to London to present on a subject I hadn't yet mastered to some very high-powered people! So this time around, I was happy to be calling in a favour.

I set off on the six-hour journey up to Peter's farm in Cumbria as the weather was starting to turn one autumn morning. There was a noticeable chill in the air and the leaves on the trees turned from deep green to golden brown as I headed north. When I arrived at his farm, Peter was there with a smile to greet me. We caught up on our news as we wandered round his 60 acres of woodland, checking out his pigs and wild boars, as well as the sheep and chickens wandering happily in the pastures. You can trace Peter's history through his farm – the impressive cheese-making equipment harks back to his successful dairy production days in the 1980s and the land is home to around a hundred animals, a menagerie that he has built up gradually and with much careful thought. But one of the best things about spending time on Peter's farm is being able to watch his pigs and compare their behaviour to that of my lot. From my trips up to Peter's I had learnt what to do when a pig gives birth and the signs to look out for when she's about to. I'll never forget the day we came across a wild boar sow giving birth in the woodland – time seemed to stand still as I watched at a distance, feeling like David Attenborough. At this time of year, however, the issue of the day was how sudden seasonal changes in the climate affect the pigs. They can handle any weather but they find it difficult to adapt

OPPOSITE AND BELOW Happy, free-ranging animals produce meat that has unbeatable succulence and flavour. Try rare-breed pork and you'll never want to eat the intensively reared stuff again.

when it changes quickly, often developing pneumonia when it does. So I learnt how to watch out for the tell-tale signs and how to administer an antibiotic injection to a pig coming down with a cough or a fever.

We spent the evening in Peter's cosy farmhouse, sinking bottles of wine, talking about the loss of the great farming traditions and dreaming of how we were going to make them great again. It is always fascinating talking to Peter. He's a bastion of traditional Englishness and his knowledge seems so endless that I think he should be a national treasure! He knows everything about every type of British food, so we chewed the fat early into the small hours and hit the hay having put the world of British food production to rights once again.

In the morning we rose with the cockerels. Peter's partner Christine made a mean fry-up with more bacon and eggs than I'd ever seen and we set to work on full bellies. In Peter's gleaming white prep room, I learnt how to bone and skin pigs, chop the meat into proper cuts and make sausages – squeezing, looping, twisting and tying all to a rhyme that Peter just couldn't get me to master! We even started to cure and slice our own bacon. It was great fun and I got an enormous sense of satisfaction as I mastered a skill that was new for me, but that been crafted and passed on over the centuries. I set off the next day, empowered by my new knowledge, and with the idea of buying some more pigs from Peter and a plan to come back to make samples for Henrietta Green to boot!

When the first pigs arrived on the farm, we housed them in the outbuildings we'd repaired and in the courtyard that Dolly had walled off for us, but by the middle of the season, we had between thirty and forty rare-breed pigs and they needed a bit more space. We moved them to another field that was too far away from the outbuildings we'd been using, so some new shelter was called for. It had to be easily accessible, very strong, clean and dry, as well as able to blend in with the landscape. With our dwindling budget, it also had to be cheap! We decided to build our own pigsties out of straw bales, pallets and the odd fence post. We stacked up the bales, bashed in some left-over fencing posts and a pallet either side to hold the straw rigid and filled the gaps between the slats with more straw. Then we left a gap for a doorway and put even more straw on the floor and finally some tin on the roof. Simple. The only obstacles we had were the playful pigs themselves. As soon as you bring something different into their environment, they're keen to find out what you're up to. They loved nothing better than knocking over the straw bales as we tried to build them. The piglets would snatch a mouthful of straw and throw it on to the grass or run around in circles to try and join in with the game. But once we'd manage to construct their new homes, they seemed quite happy with them and, as pigs do, they kept them immaculately clean. We knew that their houses would need replacing in a few months' time as the bales got wet and the barley seeds germinated, but with the bales at a pound a piece, we planned to re-build the shelters twice a year and move them and the pigs around.

OPPOSITE The first sausages I ever made certainly brought a smile to my face. A mixture of top-quality pork, onion and herbs was finely chopped, then pushed through a funnel into a prepared casing that looked far too skinny to make chubby sausages, but was actually perfect. The result was fantastic.

I was learning fast and soon feeding and looking after pigs felt like second nature. They are creatures of habit and surprisingly savvy timekeepers: they expected to see me at roughly the same time, twice a day, for food and water and they scolded me when I was late! It wasn't just the food – they also enjoyed the attention, and loved it if I took the time at mealtimes to talk, tickle and play because, as poor old Blaze had shown us when we put him on his own, they like company and need mental stimulation. There are lots of misconceptions about pigs – like the erroneous idea that they're dirty and stupid – but one thing that is true is that they love their food and will eagerly eat absolutely everything you give them, seemingly without ever becoming full. My pig feed contains things such as barley and soya proteins to fatten the pigs up naturally as well as giving them vital nutrients. As with most ready-made pig feed, it doesn't come cheap. With the amount of pigs I keep, it costs a whopping £175 a ton and we get through a ton of the stuff in an average week, although it is cheaper than mixing up and soaking our own barley meal and porridge oats as I discovered early on in my pig-keeping. I managed to run out of feed and didn't have a thing to give my hungry herd, so I dashed down to Tesco and bought up all their bags of porridge oats, which we then mixed up with milk – all the pigs had the most luxurious breakfast of freshly made porridge which was nice for them but not so good for the economics! We supplemented the Pig Nuts with potatoes and carrots bought from local farmers and, of course, other natural goodies like hazelnuts, acorns, wild mushrooms, chestnuts and apples that the pigs forage for themselves at this time of year.

Piglets everywhere

Once all the new sties were ready, we were able to take on some more livestock, so I cracked on with putting up some more fencing, while Rick took the truck up to Peter's, towing the trailer, to collect five new pigs. Luckily for me, I had a friend come and help me get the job done. Dr. Marc Cooper is an old mate of mine and a very talented one at that. He's an animal-welfare officer who inspects farms for welfare standards and is always working, so we hadn't seen each other for months. As we set to work on getting the perimeter fencing up, we chatted for hours. Good job, as this is one monotonous task – one person has to bash in the post as the other one holds the wire straight to be tacked on. The job took me back to the times I studied with Marc during our first degree in London: he'd be so patient and accurate and I would get frustrated with waiting and always want to speed things up – he'd scowl at me as I ruined his experiments by rushing on. We found ourselves in fits of laughter now as Marc carefully pondered the exact straightness of the wire as I held it, shouting 'Just hit it!' time and time again.

By the afternoon and a long line of fencing later, we decided to take a bit of a break for an hour. Besides, we could see that there was a very nice job to be done – a juicy crop

OPPOSITE Despite rumours to the contrary, pigs are very clean animals and keep their sties immaculate. A bed of fresh straw is pig heaven.

of blackberries had been twinkling at us like little shiny bullets as we tried to focus on the fencing. The fantastic weather that summer had already given us an abundance of the glossy fruit and we had decided to leave a second crop to grow, letting the natural sugars build up as the berries fattened. Now the weather was changing, it seemed a good time to give in to temptation and pull in the crop before they started to spoil. Marc and I also had the luxury of some great little helpers: Jade had a friend visit the farm after school that day and we set them a competition to see who could pick the most blackberries. It was a tough challenge because the berries were everywhere but the girls loved the idea and soon got to work. I showed them how to pull the long entangled brambles out with a gloved hand and pull the fruit off with the other, rather than let the girls prick their arms trying to weave them in and out of the branches. We all got a few pricks and scratches – the price you pay for nature's goodies – but we let the girls win, although I have to confess that Marc and I proceeded to scoff the majority of the delicious berries before getting back to the fencing. We did have a good excuse though – blackberries deteriorate quickly after they've been picked, so wash them carefully to avoid bruising and use them soon after to whip up a lovely compote, crumble, jelly, jam or whatever you fancy. And remember to prune your bushes back in the autumn to ensure another good crop next year.

Meanwhile, up in Cumbria, Peter had prepared two Tamworths, a wild boar cross and a British Lop (all rare breeds) for Rick to bring back to the farm. Using the old bucket-of-food-and-a-hungry-pig technique, Rick eventually managed to tempt the pigs into his trailer. It must have been a huge relief when he finally succeeded; pigs are awkward animals to move, especially when they don't want to. The British Lops are big white pigs,

BELOW Without exception, everyone of our new piglets were characters. Occasionally we to hand-rear some of them and those ones inevitably wormed their way into our affections.

impressive animals, and, although they are usually gentle by nature, both Lops were heavily pregnant. They seemed keener on the idea of nest-making than going on a journey but Rick took things slowly and calmly and they walked on to the trailer without a fight. In contrast, the wild boar wasn't just wild – she was livid and Rick had more than a little trouble wrestling with her. She was typically agile, strong and full of nouse and, just to show Rick who was boss, would run past the truck rather than on to it as he tried to coax her in. But good ol' Rick made it safely back to the farm with his cargo. It was great to have new rare breeds on the farm – they added colour. The pigs all looked spectacularly different and they had their own personalities as well. We called the Tamworths Tammy and Wynette and found them to be cheeky chappies and very friendly indeed. They loved a stroke and always walked over to greet me when I was in their pen, rolling over for a good scratch. The pregnant Lop, called Ethel, turned out to be the sweetest pig you could meet. She was a good old girl, placid and a bit of a loner, who would turn her head and trundle over when you called her name. She quietly got on well with pigs and humans alike, including the more outgoing and boisterous Saddleback Patricia and especially the equally calm Rick. With all the new characters on the farm, it really felt as though it was coming alive. And there was promise of new life too: Peter had said that Ethel and Patricia were about to give birth any day.

With hindsight, I think that Mr Gott may have been spinning us a bit of a yarn. He had told me that Ethel and Patricia were due to give birth and stressed that it was important to listen out for the big event. The pigs would make quite a bit of noise and knock things about a bit as they went into labour, he warned. So for days Rick and I kept rushing over to

the barn to check up on them like a couple of clucky mother hens. We had made the Lops and Saddlebacks cosy places to farrow away from their usual sty, packed with straw bedding. At night, I would jump out of bed and run out of the caravan every time I heard a noise, just in case the pigs needed help when they went into labour. But weeks passed and nothing happened (other than a lot of disturbed sleep and unnecessary worry!). We knew that a sow is pregnant for exactly three months, three weeks and three days but, of course, we had no idea of the date of conception. Then, one grey autumnal afternoon, we peeped in to check up on Ethel, and there she was, huddled with one tiny pink piglet. By the end of the day there were another three, not many for a pig of her breed, but I felt as proud as a dad to see the first litter on the farm. And, for the record, it all happened very very quietly!

A few days later Patricia went into labour and this time we were there to witness the birth. She got fidgety a few hours before she was due, re-built her nest, got fidgety again and finally settled down and waited for the piglets to come. We gave the girl lots of room and let events unfold naturally, just checking that she wasn't about to roll over and squash the newly born piglets in discomfort as others were born. A couple of hours passed and Patricia was finally able to rest, surrounded by eight healthy piglets, in her straw bed.

A few days after the birth, Ethel's litter took their first few steps and were ready to see the big outside world. We slowly introduced them to the farm, taking the mother and her piglets for a walk as the weak autumn sun shone on to the crunchy fallen leaves. Before too long, Patricia's piglets were old enough to join in and we started to turn them all out to live in the field full-time. The piglets would run and jump around excitedly, rolling around in the mud created by the rain showers, squeaking and grunting. It was plain to see that they loved their freedom, but even young piglets are clever and you

OPPOSITE I always made sure I gave new pigs the once over when they arrived at the farm.

LEFT A brave piglet ventures forth towards the edge of the wood.

could almost see them gather like naughty kids, ready to make mischief. They would look for holes in our fencing and escape, running across the fields with the dogs and often ending up at a neighbour's gate. You could almost see them thinking, 'Boy, that was fun, what can we do next?' as they ganged up like a bunch of hooligans. Off we'd run, chasing after them to rugby-tackle them in the woods and carry the rascals back home. When they got too big, we had to pen them into the chicken field with Ethel and Patricia so that they could run around, play and not get into too much trouble. The chickens, however, didn't look too chuffed. You could see the biggest cockerel, a tall 'Jack the lad' of a Maran, who up to now had ruled the roost, look noticeably miffed as the little monsters invaded his field and he realised he couldn't control them. He tried to assert his authority by strutting his stuff and upping the volume on his cock-a-doodle-doos, but the pigs ignored him. Once a day or so passed, they all seemed to be happy sharing the same space and the pigs protected the chickens against poaching foxes at night.

Separating piglets from their mother, however, wasn't so easy. It was important to wean the young ones off Ethel before they took too much sustenance from her. In commercial farming they do this at a very early age, far younger than is natural. So we decided to cut in a little later on, at about twelve weeks, to be kinder to the young and wait until Ethel started to lose condition (without compromising her health, of course). But the big old Lop wasn't having any of it. We took the piglets and put them in the front field with the wild boar and put Ethel in the back field with Tammy and Wynette to regain her strength before being mated again. But Ethel could still smell her piglets, even though they were some distance away. Then, one evening, one of the kids came running out of

BELOW Erecting fences is slow and time-consuming work, but the pigs always keep me company. Each fence post has to be knocked into the ground with a heavy two-handled block. I've never been so fit in my life.

the caravan with Rick saying they had seen a pig where it shouldn't be, and we realised that Ethel and the Tamworths had ploughed straight through the wire fencing! They were on a mission to get into the chicken field and they had almost succeeded. We had no choice but to let them in and fix up the fencing in the morning. To our amazement, there wasn't a mark on Ethel – we don't know how she did it.

The pigs on the farm never ceased to amaze me. I can't believe that so many people buy into the myth that they are dirty and stupid. In fact, we had learnt during the summer that they only wallowed in mud when the sun was really hot, to protect their otherwise pale pink skins from burning. They also loved to be hosed off to keep cool and clean, and they were constantly showing us how intelligent they were. There are some pigs that you can't help but fall in love with. I'm thinking of one little chap in particular . . .

The next pig to give birth on the farm was one of the pigs that we had saved from the abattoir. She was certainly looking a lot healthier after a few weeks of freedom, food and fresh air, but the poor old Saddleback just hadn't had enough of a good life to have a healthy litter. In fact, it had been difficult to tell how pregnant she was as she was so undernourished. One morning, Rick went down to the bottom of the field to put straight some straw housing that had gone into disarray and got a surprise: inside one of the sties was the tiniest little piglet huddled up on its own. He thought it strange that there was just one newborn, all alone, with no sow in sight, so off he went to hunt for the rest of the litter and the pig. At the bottom of the meadow, where we had dug out a couple of pools for the pigs to wallow in, Rick saw another newborn piglet on the bank of a pool. It appeared to be stuck in the mud. He carefully picked it up and walked back up the field

with the piglet in his arms to put the little one back into the farrowing pen with the other, then went off in search of its mother, calling me out to help. We soon spotted the missing mother but she had wandered off to the wood. She had turned her back on her two little piglets and, as a result, they had very little energy. If they were going to survive, they needed warmth and milk. I decided to scoop them up, carefully put them in a cardboard box stuffed with straw and bring them up to the caravan to see if a night indoors might see them through. Michaela and I were determined that the piglets would live but, to be honest, I didn't hold out much hope – they just didn't seem strong enough.

We awoke early the next morning, keen to check up on the piglets, and hurried over to the cardboard box. We were both surprised and shocked to see that there was just one piglet there – she was cold and stiff and must have died during the night. We quickly scoured the room and found the other little chap shivering in a corner. This piglet was only about as long as my foot but, unlike his weak sister, he seemed incredibly strong. A hard-nosed pig farmer may have taken the decision to hand-rear a female pig as a future breeder, but he would never bother with a male – yet we didn't have to heart to destroy him. We called him Jasper.

At first we didn't know what to feed the little pig so he got a luxury start of tepid gold-top milk, which he loved Michaela to feed him with a bottle while he was cradled in her arms. We discovered that we could buy replacement sow's milk from the vet and Jasper responded to it quickly, gaining strength in what seemed to be an equal proportion to character! While he was very tiny, Jasper lived in the caravan, sleeping in a cardboard box and running up and down excitedly, squealing with pleasure when Michaela came

BELOW Our piglets grew from tiny animals into big and boisterous pigs who had very winning ways.

home at the end of each day. In the evenings he would sit with Michaela and the dogs on the Barbie-pink sofa as we all watched TV. He would nudge himself into a cosy corner, nestling up to Cora the terrier, and fall asleep. I'd sit on the floor, watching his eyes grow heavy as he nodded off, thinking 'Hang on, I've got this wrong somewhere!' For a while, Jasper lived almost like a pet but he got very boisterous, running around and knocking things over. You can't expect a pig to be completely house trained! We were keen to give him a normal life and integrate him with the other pigs, but we knew that he would have to do it gradually.

As soon as Jasper was big and strong enough, we started to put him out in the field for a few hours at a time to see how he would fare. The tiny runt would have a good snort about, a bit of a dig, a bit of a burrow, but soon find a way to escape and wander back to the caravan door. He would wait there to be let in, or follow Michaela around, grunting continuously, demanding that she feed him. When he was bigger still, we decided to put Jasper in the field with the dogs, to live with them in the kennel for a while. He made friends with Parker, Rick's Jack Russell cross, and seemed to love running around with the dogs that he used to snooze with on our couch. But Jasper was essentially a pig, with pig intelligence and instinct, so we shouldn't have been surprised to discover that he was causing all sorts of mischief on the quiet.

One day I decided to watch Jasper to see exactly what he got up to. I discovered that as soon as we let him out of the dog kennel first thing in the morning, he would run into the barn where the pig feed was kept. He hid behind the straw bales and sat there for as long as no one noticed, happily troughing his way through the big pile of grain. Then he took a stroll over to turn out all of the rubbish bins, or dig up the garden in search of more food, before returning to that ready-made pile. No wonder he was putting on weight! He was a right monkey, always in trouble, but you couldn't help but like the little chap all the more for his antics. But, for the time being, I had more pressing things on my mind.

All the fun of the fair

Henrietta Green's Food Lovers' Fair was creeping closer by the day and I had to get some sample sausages over to the lady herself to secure our stall. We had planned another expedition up to Peter's farm in Cumbria to make them but, before Rick and I could set off, we had to send our first pigs to slaughter.

We wanted to make the whole process as humane as possible and had taken our time to visit and find the right abattoir for the job. Regulations mean that all animals have to be slaughtered on licensed premises. We eventually found a small local business that had been operating on the same site for four generations. I liked their traditional approach, the fact that they didn't hurry the pigs and made the process as comfortable

for them as possible. Commercial pressures have meant that this kind of abattoir is hard to find today and, unsurprisingly, some welfare standards have dropped. My friend Marc, the animal-welfare officer, had told me all sorts of horror stories of what can happen in the big abattoirs, where speed and cost come before the animals; he's seen pigs shoved on to conveyor belts in droves. But there is no need for this treatment and if people knew more about it, they would undoubtedly protest at such methods. Who wants to save a few pennies at the cost of this kind of stress and suffering? At this abattoir they seemed to look after the pigs until the very end. When the pigs arrived, they were held in a pen and allowed time to settle down; then they were moved one at a time and properly stunned before being quickly killed away from the others. After that, the carcasses were handled in the most professional and swift way. It set my mind at rest and I felt my pigs would be properly treated, so we went down there with three of our nice fat pigs. I drove the pigs in the trailer. We were then going to return in the afternoon with the refrigerated van to pick up the carcasses. As a sign of respect to the poor old pigs that we took down there that day, we finally removed the rings from their noses and buried them on the farm – at least symbolically, they were free.

Up at Peter's, the pressure was on. We only had a couple of days before the Fair and we had to make a ton of sausages and fast! Rick couldn't believe the difference in butchering the rare-breed meat compared to the intensively farmed pigs he'd trained on. He marvelled at the difference – the rich colour of our pigs' meat and its texture with a natural juicy layer of fat (a sign of sweetness, and where the taste is). He discovered that the odd black bristle in the meat, a sign of quality, replaced the bruised joints and abscesses he was used to. The bruises are a product of commercial pigs being kept in a confined indoor space and being knocked about as they scramble to feed; the abscesses are often a sign of illness or disease.

It was great to see our first, very own sausages appear. We made them from the shoulder and leg of pork rather than the sinew and other junk you'll find in most mass-produced sausages and, because of this, they boast a minimum of 93 per cent meat content. We use a little bit of rusk to bind our sausages together in the true British tradition. Rusk is important to the eating quality of a sausage, but it's got bad press in recent years. This is borne out of unscrupulous butchers padding their sausages with far too much rusk and not enough meat, but it is a question of balance – the right amount of rusk makes a sausage taste less dense and doesn't compromise its flavour. There are those, though, who love a full meaty flavour and for them we now make a 100 per cent meat sausage. It's a very European recipe, the only ingredients being cured bacon, fresh pork and a sprinkling of seasoning. We made a few different varieties of sausage for Henrietta Green's Food Lovers' Fair: as well as the standard pork sausage there was the Autumn Sausage, made by adding our own freshly picked chestnuts and apples from the

OPPOSITE **Pigs are very friendly and affectionate animals. They enjoy company and really love having their ears or back scratched.**

farm, along with bay leaves and seasoning and the Cambridge Sausage, made from a recipe including nutmeg and ginger, which dates back to 1917 and has been used by traditional butchers ever since. We also added a Beer Sausage for some seasonal fun. With our own streaky bacon, as well as some Saddleback dry-cured bacon, we were just about ready for the event.

Our sausages and bacon didn't feel quite like our own without The Essex Pig Company labels and packaging, but they tasted fantastic. So we shipped a few off to Henrietta Green at the very last minute and waited for her response. Everybody was delighted when she came back to us with a firm 'Delicious!' – we would be going to the Fair. We also prepared some bacon, and collected chestnuts in the woodland to sell too – all with just a day to go before the Fair!

Just to make things even more complicated, I had to nip off to Norfolk the next morning to collect some pigs that I'd seen advertised for sale from a man called Mark Priest. I left Asa and Rick to prepare the finishing touches for the Fair that grey morning while I drove up to Mark's farm. It was a rush against the clock so, inevitably, I got lost! By the time I was meant to be at the farm, I found myself deep in the East Anglian Fenns with no idea of where I was, other than in the middle of nowhere, and no reception on my mobile to call Mark for help. After a few more miles of driving around frantically, looking for a road sign or street name I could match to my map, I spotted some locals. A couple of old boys in flat caps put me back on track and I arrived at the farm in no time. Mark Priest wanted to sell off all of his pigs – two lovely Saddleback sows that were both pregnant, three big Gloucester Old Spots, and a poor boar that was about to go for the chop. I felt a bit sorry for the big chap, so I ended up taking five home, leaving Mark with just one prized Old Spot, his favourite. Although I managed to avoid another map-reading mishap on the way back, I arrived home late with the pigs, put the boar in the shed and the females in the field.

The next morning we fed the animals as usual, double-checked that we had everything in order for the Fair, and set off for Covent Garden in the afternoon. It was going to be our first-ever outing as The Essex Pig Company and I was keen to get things right. So Rick, Asa and I set off in good time to arrive early that evening and set up the stall in advance of the big day. We were taking no risks.

Everything went according to plan. We parked up, put our products into the cold storage provided for the night, and set up our stall and the tarpaulin next to Peter's stand. By 9.30pm we'd cracked it, so we went to Asa's flat were we were spending the night. We dumped our bags and headed off to the pub for last orders. I don't know quite how it happened, perhaps it was the excitement of being back in the big city, but one drink seemed to lead to another and we all ended up a bit worse for wear. Suddenly we were in The Roadhouse, listening to live bands until three in the morning! Nevertheless, we still managed to get up at six as planned, all a bit groggy, with Rick looking decidedly green around the gills as he gulped down a bottle of water. We had two busy days of trading ahead of us.

Henrietta Green's Food Lovers' Fair was like no other farmers' market I'd ever been to. There were around forty stalls in the elegant Covent Garden courtyard designed by the great architect Inigo Jones, selling some of the best British food around. The traders had travelled from all over the country and their colourful stalls stocked all sorts of wonderful things, from ostrich meat to the finest hand-made chocolates. There was a bustling, carnival atmosphere as Londoners, tourists, foodies and passers-by milled around and rolled up to the stalls, a reggae band playing behind us. Rick, Asa and I soon got our traders' spiel going and we nobbled two dodgy Elvis impersonators who were busking nearby and bribed them with some sausages to shout out, 'The Essex Pig Company' as they danced in their high white collars and big glasses. We built up a good rapport with the punters, trade was brisk and the stall became swamped when Jamie, who's as passionate about quality food as I am, came down to help flog some bacon.

Then I got a call on my mobile. Amid all of the chaos, I could hardly hear the voice on the end of the line, but it was Michaela – and she was in trouble. The new boar we had put in the shed on the farm had smelt one of the sows in the field that was in season and was trying to break out of the shed doors and was determined to get to her. Frightened and panicky, Michaela said that only she and Lynn were on the farm and they didn't know how they would stop the big beast! I told Michaela not to try and stop the boar, but just let him into the field, because he would make his way there anyway and probably cause all sorts of damage along the way. To add to the drama, after we had put the phone down, the sow somehow managed to escape and was heading for the shed. Michaela and Lynn wrestled with the pig and eventually coaxed her back to the field, then they quickly

LEFT **We made four different types of sausage for Henrietta Green's Food Lovers' Fair in Covent Garden. They all went down a treat.**

opened the shed door that the boar was now head-butting and let him stampede over to her. It must have been pretty frightening – he was huge and very forceful! Just hours after the ordeal, Michaela and Lynn arrived at the Fair to help us trade the next day, and regaled us with tales of how they had turned around to shut the gate on the boar and the sow, only to see the boar running towards them! They made a hasty exit.

Day two of the Food Lovers' Fair was just as exciting as the first. There seemed to be even more people visiting the event and we saw lots of familiar faces too. There were Michaela's friends Des and Anna, some of my mates, and my mum and dad. At one point, it felt as though there were more of us behind the stall than punters in front of it! Mum, bless her, thought we would need some sandwiches and brought a load down in her Tupperware containers – to the Food Fair! As for The Essex Pig Company, we got off to a flying start. Things couldn't have gone any better – our products were a real hit and we made a profit. In fact, we sold clean out of sausages by lunchtime and packed up early, tipping our white butchers' hats to Peter Gott as we headed back to the farm. We were exhausted but all the hard work and preparation had been worth it. Even better, I had renewed faith that we were doing the right thing and that the farm would be what I'd dreamed of.

To market, to market

Things on the farm were changing – the weather was turning decidedly chillier and the days were starting to grow shorter by the time Lynn moved into Rick's caravan at Halloween. We moved some of the pigs into the middle of the paddock and, before too long, they discovered the orchard. Amid the thick nettles and bramble bushes, I could trace the little paths that the pigs had ploughed, leading to huge apple and hazelnut trees, heavy with fruit. The land all around the trees had been flattened by the pigs as they hoovered up and scoffed the windfalls. I've never seen such happy-looking animals. They were in pig heaven!

But life on the farm wasn't all about pigs. While the weather was reasonably good, we pushed on with setting up the farm shop. Inspired by the Food Lover's Fair and all of the positive e-mails we'd received from happy punters afterwards, we were keen to produce more of our sausages and bacon and sell them on-line as well as at local farmers' markets. The website, www.essexpigcompany.com, had been designed by my cousin Amy and was now up and running so we were almost in a position to get going. We made a big effort to get the shop to the stage where it could be used as a processing plant, fixing the leaking roof and installing the necessary equipment. Then we had our hard work checked by the Health Authority and, with enormous relief, got the green light to start producing our own products on-site. It was a real and important turning point for The Essex Pig Company.

We planned to get ourselves a regular circuit of stalls at a couple of local farmers' markets each week by the onset of winter, so Michaela and I started to visit a variety of markets every weekend, to see which would be right for us and to check out the competition. I love markets. I love their tradition and their community spirit – people still use them as a meeting place and you can see a few old boys drinking tea in the market square every week, as well as young mums gathering to buy their fruit and veg, stopping to have a chat with a few stall holders along the way. They're also a brilliant link between the consumer and producer, you know what you're buying is locally grown and there is a pride in both the buying and the selling. Make sure you seek out farmers' markets that focus on quality produce and where a lot of the food will be fresh, if you want to take home the best fresh food in town.

If you're lucky, you can find a farmers' market that's close to where you live and is held weekly or twice weekly, and you don't need to be in the country to do so. In the major cities, many markets are held in traditional locations, built years ago for the purpose, such as Borough Market in Bermondsey, south London. Other smaller markets can be found in car parks or behind leisure centres all over the country. You just need to keep your eyes peeled, or flick to my list of farmers' markets around the country on page 217. They seem to be springing up everywhere at the moment, but some are only a monthly event, which means they can only be enjoyed as an occasional interest rather

BELOW The golden autumn days brought with them a wealth of nature's goodies. The pigs loved nothing more than gorging on windfall apples, nuts and acorns.

than a way of life. I've even seen some farmers' markets set up in supermarket car parks – an interesting juxtaposition. The thing is that you can't expect the farmer who produces his own food to be able to compete with supermarket prices – and therein lies the rub. At the first local farmers' market we traded at after the Food Lovers' Fair, we were met with a mixed reaction. Some customers thought our sausages and bacon were above the average price one would expect in say one of the major supermarkets.I explained about how our sausages and bacon were made and the old adage rang true - you get what you pay for! If our bacon takes three months to produce (plus eight months to prepare the pig) then the price has to reflect the process, not what you could buy off the supermarket shelf instead. The commercial timeline of intensively farmed animals is just so different. Whereas once a market stocked goods at discounted prices and was a place to pick up a bargain, the farmers' market is all about being able to pick up the best quality: home-grown vegetables, meats, fish, cheeses and bread. And for that pleasure we need to get used to paying a bit more for good food. A lot of the food in this country is bad and cheap, because cost is what the consumer has traditionally responded to. But we're being lied to with words like 'farm' and 'fresh' and 'homemade' and palmed off with shoddy products and nasty food. People who used to adulterate food in the old days were put in the stocks, or hanged! We need to change our attitudes and make good food a priority that is worth paying a little extra for – believe me, it will make an incredible difference.

Out in the vegetable patch

As I mentioned in the last chapter, there is also a way to get quality produce on your table without the cost and have a bit of fun along the way. You can't beat eating food that you've grown yourself. You just can't compare what you can buy in the shops with the flavour of freshly picked autumn fruits or veggies.

Autumn is a great time for harvesting, which is why, of course, it is the time of the Harvest Festival, when the gathering in of the crops was celebrated with thanksgiving in church and a slap-up meal afterwards. As the summer fruits and vegetables come to an end, a whole new harvest of delicious things appears. This is the time to trundle indoors with a box heavy with fresh goodies from a few hours well spent in the garden. Apples should be ripe and ready to store – just pick all the rubbish off them and wrap only perfect ones in paper and put them away somewhere cool and dark. It's best to eat the rest, as apples with bruises, stalks missing or any other minor damage, won't store well. The apples that you buy in the supermarket are usually stored for about a year before they hit the shelves, so your freshly picked ones, despite the odd spot or bruise, should taste much, much better.

This is also the time to pull in your root crops. Now I call these grandad crops because they remind me of going down to an allotment and seeing fifty carrots planted in

OPPOSITE **It gave us all huge pleasure to see the pigs snuffling happily around ground that we'd laboured so hard to clear.**

ABOVE Growing things, whether plants or animals is immensely satisfying. The vegetable patch we planted on the farm kept us supplied with the basics throughout the autumn and winter.

nice, neat rows by some old chap. I remember watching Percy Thrower on *Blue Peter* when I was a kid and he was great, but he used to tell you all of the rules to obey and I never really had the time or I didn't want to take the fun out of it and follow all of the guidelines. I would recommend you grow vegetables that you eat regularly, depending on your taste, rather than grow for growing's sake. For example, I prefer young, tasty, lighter vegetables to big old cabbages and cauliflowers. I'd rather throw down some rocket seeds, let nature take care of itself and eat rocket leaves throughout the year, than rush out on the 6th October to pull up my line of carrots – not least because nature doesn't work in straight lines! I do love a pumpkin, though, or squash and, although they are mostly grown in more warmer climates, if you have a sunny, south-facing garden you can do really well with them. If you're harvesting yours this autumn, you should check out Gennaro's pumpkin risotto recipe on page 198.

One of the plants that I've re-discovered a passion for recently is rhubarb. I love this kind of pure, simple food that has been around for years and surprises you with how good it is when you taste it again. Rhubarb used to have a reputation as a grandad crop and was always just served with custard or in a crumble when I was a kid, but now it's used brilliantly in sweet and savoury dishes. And it's easy to grow as well – plant in the late autumn and you'll have a crop the following spring to enjoy. Rhubarb can be grown in most soil and, once established, it will need very little attention. To get it to that stage, you need to put in a little bit of graft early on. I would recommend that you work well-rotted manure or compost deep into the soil, about twice the depth usually needed for most vegetables because the roots of a rhubarb plant like to penetrate deeply. Then, about a month before planting, dig a hole of approximately 2-feet square for each root to be dropped into. In October or November, put a little more compost or manure at the bottom of each hole before pushing the root on top. Then fill up around the root with another shovelful of manure and finally a spread of topsoil. You want to keep your root covered but leave any new shoots to protrude. Tread in the soil around the roots with your feet and water it if it's dry. If you're planting more than one root, just leave about a two feet between each one to develop a patch. A great thing about rhubarb is that it gives you a fruit crop at the beginning of the year, when most varieties aren't ready and you're otherwise relying on your store apples.

Autumn is also the perfect opportunity to get out in your garden and enjoy the last of the weather while you prepare the soil for the onset of winter and growth dormancy – that is, when plants shut down their resources and go to sleep. Dormancy is a gardener's mate and now is the time to capitalise on it, however small your patch. If you dig up a plant, split it (cut it in half) and re-plant it, you will be able to grow two of equal size, if not bigger, from each half by the end of your season, doubling your crop. You can do the same with bulbs but you need to do this when the plant is dormant rather than when it is concentrating on flowering, producing seed or shooting up from the roots. If you dig it up while it's all singing and dancing, then it will suffer. So do it now and, by the time spring kicks in, the roots on both halves will become active and you'll have really, healthy, happy plants.

Puppy love

It wasn't just pigs that we acquired on the farm that autumn; we added to our collection of dogs too. Rick had waited almost two years for one of his friends to breed his chocolate-brown Labrador and his springer spaniel to form 'springerdor' pups and Rick had always promised himself one or two when his friend succeeded. News came that the puppies had indeed arrived. Now that Rick lived on the farm full-time, he loved the idea of having a dog he could train to work on the farm and take shooting. He was keen to go and see the puppies. While he was up there, I got an excited call to say that the little ones were in great shape and he hoped to have two. Rick sounded very excited about the dogs and I thought it would be a good idea to adopt one as a surprise for Michaela and asked if there was a big male who looked like he might grow up to have enough presence as a guard dog on the farm. Rick said he'd seen just the chap and the deal was done. Now we waited for Mark to deliver them to us and we all agreed to keep their arrival as a surprise for Michaela.

We already had some great four-legged characters on the farm. There was Parker, Rick's friendly Jack Russell cross, Bracken, my placid old spaniel, and Cora, my tearaway terrier. But it was the perfect environment for more – they had acres to romp around, could get plenty of exercise and have a great life outdoors.

I wasn't there the day the puppies were delivered but I heard that all notions of their being outdoor dogs went out of the window as soon as they arrived! They turned up wrapped in a blanket with their mother's smell on it and Lynn and Jade took one look at their little shivering female pup, Lady, and the little chap, Prince, and fell for them. They bundled them up and took them straight inside the caravan along with Michaela's puppy until she came home. Rick was a bit miffed – he thought the dogs should be outside with the others and didn't fancy sharing the already tiny living space with two dogs, two kids and another adult when the dogs had their own kennel; but Lynn wanted the puppies to be house-trained and promised Rick that they would sleep outside once they were. When I got back to the farm, I called Michaela at work and told her that her puppy would be there when she got home. The last time I had heard her sound so excited was when I called to tell her that we had hot water in the caravan!

Michaela rushed back to the farm that night and I met her with a tiny chocolate-brown puppy, which I presented to her from behind my back. She fell in love with him instantly and called him Woody. Even I have to admit he was a very handsome dog, with a playful personality and the brightest green eyes. I already had my dogs, so it was great that Michaela could have her own and that he would grow up to be a big strong guard dog for the farm. She started to train Woody immediately and loved playing around with him; they became inseparable.

As soon as the puppies were big enough, they all went to sleep outside in the kennels with the other dogs and really got to know each other. It was interesting to see how they formed little cliques – Bracken seemed to be in charge of the spaniel-type dogs (including Woody, Lady and Prince) who never strayed far from the farm, while Cora and Parker, the terriers, would always be up to something or off on an adventure. Cora was intelligent and very much the quiet boss of all of the dogs even though she was one of the smallest. I remember that it was around this time that she started to take great interest in the chicks on the farm. She would sit in the field and watch them, quite innocently, but you'd think, 'Well, what's she up to?' After twenty or so minutes she'd wait until the chicks turned a corner, follow them and you'd notice later that there were a couple fewer! She was a real sly one.

Party time

As usual there was lots to do on the farm as well as look after the animals. When we set out on this adventure, we knew that it wouldn't be easy but we did hope for a

relatively quiet life on the farm. There was always something happening, though, and this autumn, Michaela was organising the biggest event we'd held yet.

Two years before, just after Christmas 2001, Michaela's dad passed away as a result of motor neurone disease. Michaela took the decision to do something positive in his memory – she planned to raise money for the Motor Neurone Disease Association, a charity which funds research into the disease. Michaela planned to hold a big event that she would call 'On Fire' at the farm. This would combine a charity auction to raise money, a huge bonfire, fireworks and a barbecue to create some seasonal fun, not least because the event, to be held in early November, also fell on her sister Charlie's birthday. It was a huge responsibility and was going to be a lot of work, but the two sisters joined forces and together they set about organising this very significant event.

They worked hard on their idea for two or three months, planning every little detail and using all of their contacts to make it happen. Charlie's boyfriend's brother was an events organiser, so he booked some bands to play live in the barn and rigged up the lighting that would be their backdrop. Another of Charlie's friends was in catering and agreed to take care of the food and roped in a brewery to donate the drink, while someone else built a website and organised the tickets. I provided sausages, asked Peter Gott to supply us with a hog roast for the barbecue, and my friend, the talented chef Gennaro, offered to make some of his delicious homemade soup.

I first met Gennaro through Jamie. We instantly hit it off and soon realised that we

ABOVE It often seems that pigs never stop eating. When not feasting on the pig cereal I buy at huge expense, they're always grubbing around looking for snacks.

both share a passion for wildlife and nature. Gennaro is incredibly warm and generous and full of Italian spirit. He often buys me beautiful old books on nature and food and has taken me to Italy to experience rural olive-oil tasting. His restaurant *Passione*, in central London, is one of my favourite places to eat. You can often find the wonderful wild mushrooms and rare squashes that he tells me all about on the menu, or displayed on a table outside the restaurant, like exotic flowers, for passers-by to marvel at.

With the help of friends, family and colleagues, Michaela and Charlie covered every detail of the event and left nothing to chance. They bought hay bales, borrowed gas heaters from a neighbouring farm, made and bought decorations for the barn, and set up a stage. They even ordered a huge delivery of gravel to lay in front of the farm shop which, after a few downpours, turned into a slippery mud bath. I remember Michaela nervously checking the five-day weather forecast on-line, muttering, 'Please don't rain, please don't rain' as the big day approached. Michaela spent the whole weekend before the party clearing out the barn which, remember, used to be the biggest in Suffolk!

The day before the party, Michaela's folks set up camp in a cottage nearby to hold a family reunion. Michaela's mum flew over from France, her brother travelled from Gibraltar, and they were joined by Michaela's cousins, her sister Charlie and Charlie's boyfriend. My mum and dad came too and both families got stuck in, working hard alongside friends to make sure that the event was both successful and professional, fulfilling everything the invitations had promised and everything the girls had envisioned. Together with Michaela's friends Des and Anna, everyone ran around putting up decorations and props, creating a haunted house in the derelict farmhouse (complete with pumpkin lanterns) and making hundreds of phone calls to ensure the deliveries would arrive on time the next day. Parking was cordoned off in the field, balloons were blown up and tied to the gateposts, and signs were made to lead everyone to the party. On the morning of the big event, an army of friends and family turned up and pulled together to put the finishing touches in place and support the girls. Together they finished off the barn, helped with the decorations and set up a bar. Then all of the youngsters jumped into the van and headed for the woods to salvage logs and build a massive bonfire in the middle of one of the fields, topping it off with two enormous rotten old beams that made the fire twelve feet or more in height.

'On Fire' was a fantastic night. It was a resounding success. As all of our hard work came together and the sun set over the farm, the clear crisp evening sky turned an inky blue and we all gathered in the barn. I was bowled over to see how many people had turned up already and how great the place looked. There were neat rows of straw bales set around low tables decorated with lavender plants, chocolates and sweets, all set on top of red paper table cloth and sprinkled with gold stars. The stage was rigged with professional lights, there was a place for the DJ, and the whole spectacle was topped with

ABOVE **Gennaro Contaldo is a great friend of mind and a fantastic chef. He has a passion for fresh, wild food, which you're likely to find on the menu of his aptly named restaurant *Passione* in London's Charlotte Street.**

a big, pink, hand-painted, hanging pig! The bars were neatly stocked with tequila, wine and beer, and the trestle tables were heavy with salads, bread and other delicious food to accompany the barbecue.

The evening began with the DJ saying a few well-chosen words, then we kicked off with a silent auction. The lots of holidays to Ireland and France were chalked up on a blackboard alongside an offer of two tables at Fifteen for seven-course meals. Everyone was encouraged to step up and scribble a price to claim a prize in the silent bidding war, with the final scribbled bid winning the lot. The crowd was anything but silent, cheering and clapping the bidders – great fun. Meanwhile, it was time to get the hot soup on the go. Gennaro had sent up vast amounts of delicious broth that we warmed through on the cooker in the farm shop for people to grab on their way up to the bonfire.

The fire was an impressive sight, roaring up high into the night sky, by the time the party wandered over. It was a toasty meeting point for guests to chat, eat soup and have a bottle of beer while the drummer Michaela had hired created a festival atmosphere with his beats. Then it was time for the fireworks – big bangers, whizzers and rockets made a tremendous sight as they exploded in the sky and emblazoned it with vibrant colours.

As the booze ran dry and the fire burned low, we all rushed back to the barn to see who was winning the auction and get the barbecue underway. The hog roast, sausages and veggie treats all went down a storm and we ate while listening to some live music from Woody, the one-man band. There was more auction fun, a tarot-card reader in the haunted house, and a deluge of work colleagues and friends who turned up for the knees-up in the barn. I had to laugh at one point – while most people were queuing up for food, the DJ from Plymouth Sounds played a record as just one person got down on the dance floor. Definitely an Alan Partridge moment! But DJ Simon was fantastic, as were the live bands. My mates were impressive too – after a few more drinks, we stormed the stage, forming an impromptu band and everyone danced into the small hours. It was a real thigh-slapping shindig.

As people started to leave and the barn cleared, about ten of us huddled to chat and lark about under the gas heaters with a stereo until four in the morning, when we decided to call it a night. After just a few hours' sleep, Asa and I launched Operation Clean-up the next morning and got things back into shape on the farm. Of course we had sore heads and tired eyes, but we were happy in the knowledge that we had raised around £5,000 for a very worthy charity and had a lot of fun doing it.

Sheep ahoy

The morning after the party I was expecting our first sheep to arrive on the farm. You might think I already had enough on my plate with the chickens, geese, ducks and dogs, not to mention my ever-expanding herd of pigs. But, as I said before, I'd always wanted a farm with a variety of livestock – a real mix of animals – and sheep made sense. They are much lower maintenance than pigs and mostly look after themselves – just think of the ones you see roaming the hillsides in the Lake District or in Wales. They keep themselves to themselves for the most part, acting as extraordinarily efficient lawn mowers. Not only that, but I'd be able to offer lamb sausages in the farm shop as well and, as far as I was concerned, the more variety and interest we could tempt the punters with, the better. So I had bought five Soays, a primitive breed, from a lady and her husband in Norfolk, and I was keen to get them on the farm – they're fantastic animals. Their young produce tasty meat known as Hoggart Lamb, they are excellent mothers and, most unusually, they shed their coats naturally, which means that they never need shearing.

For all of their good points, though, Soays have a reputation for being temperamental animals – they're pretty wild and impossible to herd. So I was keen to have everything ready for their arrival and an atmosphere of calm on the farm, not least because their current owner had advised me that it was a good idea.

Asa and I managed to clear out the barn and get rid of most of the tell-tale party signs before the lady and her husband swept up the drive towing their trailer. She jumped out of the car, we said our hellos and she told me that the sheep had been a bit agitated already that morning. Then, just as we opened the trailer and I was trying to allay her fears, the unthinkable happened. Asa put what he thought was an empty cardboard box on to the bonfire, but it actually contained a load of left-over fireworks which went off like

OPPOSITE **With numerous partygoers crashed out in the caravans, we decided to cook breakfast outdoors. There's nothing quite like a fry-up of superb sausages and eggs to beat a hangover.**

ABOVE **I decided to introduce sheep to the farm as I wanted to broaden my livestock.**

gunshots across the farm! We all froze in horror. But, to my amazement, the sheep took absolutely no notice and weren't fazed a bit, which is more than I can say for the farmers, who probably thought we were the most irresponsible people they'd ever met!

A visit to the wild larder

A few days later, Gennaro popped up to visit the farm for the first time. It was fantastic to see him: even though we'd relished his soup at the bonfire party, we had missed his presence. We'd had lots of rain and floods on the farm and, as the weather lifted and the mist dissolved that morning, the woodland looked incredible. The leaves had fallen to reveal the skeletons of the trees and all of a sudden it was possible to see how many had fallen over the years. The woodland floor was a riot of colour, covered with the russet leaves that glistened with raindrops and dew. I loved watching the seasons change on the farm: it really felt as if the weather and wildlife evolved a little each day, right in front of my eyes. It also reminded me of how oblivious I had become to the seasons and the weather when working in the city. Now I could observe all the different terrain on the farm – the damp bogs, the hillocks and raised ground, the dry shady areas, the pastures, fields and woods; the stream that ran through the woodland, as well as the wildlife, wild flowers and foods that grew within it. It was always a treat to catch a glimpse of a barn owl, or tawny owl, a bat or a stoat, a weasel or a badger, a roe or a fallow deer – if you were quick, quiet and lucky. But, of course, Gennaro could always show me more and teach me a thing or two – he was a real expert on wild food. As Gennaro and I walked through the wood, catching up on each other's news, he picked up a ton of sweet chestnuts from the woodland floor. The small ones that we Brits usually disregard are preferred by the Italians because, once cooked, they're far sweeter. We also tend to avoid the little ones because they have more green spikes and our logic is typically, 'They're smaller, there's less to them and they are twice as likely to prickle me! I'll go for the big 'uns.' But once the little blighters are cracked open and cooked, they're very tasty and worth the hassle. When you're out walking in the woods at this time of year, look for the trees that bear large, long leaves with pointy ends (the trees bearing similar fruit with fewer green spikes and rounded leaves are conker trees and you don't want to be eating those!). The best way to avoid pricking your hands is to copy my trick: roll each spiky chestnut pod on the woodland floor with your feet to crack them open before picking them up. There is no better way, believe me, because whatever gloves you wear, the spikes will stick into you like hundreds of little needles.

There are several ways of cooking chestnuts: when we have a barbecue we stick them in the fire on a metal dustbin lid to roast, but you can do just as good a job if you bung them in the oven on a baking tray for half an hour or so. We also boil and peel chestnuts to add to some of our sausages; if you boil yours, make sure you split the skin with a knife first to stop them exploding. Don't panic if your water turns brown – it's just the natural tannins seeping out.

I told Gennaro that we'd sold some of our chestnuts at the Food Lovers' Fair and he nearly fainted when I told him what we'd charged for them. He thought it was incredibly cheap for so much trouble and said that he'd have bought the lot if he'd known. They are worth a small fortune. Such treats are worth storing, so that you can savour them when they are out of season. To keep chestnuts fresh, bury them in a bucket of sand and put them in a dry garage or shed and they will keep for several months. Just don't be tempted to store them in sawdust or other such material that will absorb moisture from the atmosphere and make your little gems soggy.

Another little treasure you can find foraging in the woodlands is the wild mushroom. Gennaro and I were on the look-out for a particular variety that day – the delicious Honey fungus. Honey fungus is actually a disease that trees contract. It grows around the base of the trunk of the same trees each year; it looks quite beautiful and tastes even better, but it will eventually kill the tree. For this reason, it's a real pest to gardeners but to an Italian chef, it's a goldmine. Honey fungus is one of those trendy fungi that you can pick up in an exclusive deli for a fortune, which is why pickers are guarded about where they find their mushrooms – a crop around one tree can be worth up to £70! So that afternoon Gennaro and I set about looking for some in the woodland where we could pick it for free. But a word of warning – it looks incredibly similar to a very poisonous variety of wild mushroom called Sulphur Tuft, that will make you seriously ill if you eat it. This is not an unusual story in the mushroom world. There are around 3,000 species of wild mushroom in the UK, but only about a hundred of these are edible and a handful of twenty or so are deadly, the most poisonous of which is called the death cap. My advice would be to get out there, hunt for nature's goodies and bring them back to your dinner table, but be careful how you go about it. I would suggest that you start off by picking fungi you can easily identify and know well, like oyster mushrooms, chanterelles, ceps, field mushrooms and puff balls. Avoid any mushroom that you cannot identify, and any carrying or growing from a volva bag (a cup-shaped sheath on the stalk of the mushroom which generally indicates nasty fellows). Remember to check that the mushrooms look healthy, fresh and free from parasites before you pick them and to give them a good wipe or gentle wash when you get home. As for cooking, there are many ways but you can't go wrong, even with puff balls (huge, white mushrooms that are literally the size of a football and need cutting into steaks) if you keep it simple and gently fry in olive oil, garlic and rosemary.

Gennaro and I found that the rain had spoilt the Honey fungus, but that didn't stop us from continuing our trek. We came across all sorts of things. Gennaro gathered some nettles, singing, 'Hello, I love you' to them so that, he claimed, they wouldn't sting him! But my favourites are dandelion leaves that make a great addition to a salad if picked fresh and young. Posh Elizabethans used to grow dandelions in their gardens to do the very same thing and, although they're best in spring, I couldn't resist taking a handful home.

With all of the fallen branches on the woodland floor, it was a great time to make a walking stick. It was something that I really fancied but had never done before, so Gennaro showed me how. First, find a branch with a bit of character that's no more than five feet long and is fairly straight and sturdy. Then get rid of the bits that fork off the branch by carefully cutting away twigs and forks with a sharp pocket knife (I use an Opinel), leaving the small stump of a fork at the top. Next, peel the bark carefully off the entire stick, or carve in a pattern and cut away the ends of the bark. Leave the stick to dry out overnight and when it's completely dry, it's ready to use. You can rub the whole thing down with sandpaper, wipe off any dust with a cloth and stain or varnish it to seal your stick, if you want something that really looks the business.

Gennaro and I continued to walk and chat and he told me how much he loved the farm. He loved seeing the pigs, our new way of life and the varied wildlife; he was wonderfully enthusiastic about it all. If it weren't for being able to live the dream through me, he said that he would be green with envy. But he wasn't so impressed with the fact that I rarely had time to eat lunch! He'd turned up with his own pots and pans as well as some wonderful arborio rice, took one look in my cupboards when we got back to the caravan after our walk, and said I had nothing to eat! In no time at all, Gennaro rustled up a fantastic pumpkin risotto, using the left-over pumpkins from the haunted house, and finished it off with some nettle fritters, made with the nettles he'd picked so lovingly that afternoon in the woodland. It was a delicious feast and just what we needed to warm ourselves up on a chilly autumn afternoon. The recipes are on pages 198 and 204, if you'd like to try them for yourself. It always feels good to add a little something that you've found in nature's pantry or grown yourself.

Talking of home-grown, we were still using the farm shop as a processing plant that autumn. There had been more of a pressure to get to market than to open the shop itself and our success had been fundamental to the continuing existence of The Essex Pig Company. But now we had our own products to sell, we couldn't wait to finish off the shop. It was all part of setting up and realising the dream. We had all of the equipment but no rustic charm, so we went about taking the edges off the clinical white box that we'd created. We decided that the best way would be to put in some furniture with a country feel to display the goods that didn't need to be refrigerated, so Michaela started to search for Welsh dressers, a big round table, chairs and a rug in the free ads and the

BELOW Sweet chestnuts, in their prickly green cases, are among the free treasures you can find in woodland during the autumn. Although they're fiddly to prepare, they have a fantastic flavour – and they cost a fortune in the shops.

internet. The shop needed warmth and country appeal. It would probably have to wait until after Christmas, but I was determined that, as soon as possible, we'd be open for business. . .

By the end of autumn, our second season, I was beginning to feel established on the farm. We had a large stock of animals now, who were already providing us with food both to sell and to enjoy; my vegetable garden was yielding up produce and there was all the wild bounty in the woods as well. I had a daily routine of hard work that varied depending on what needed doing, or what was coming up that week. As the days grew cooler and shorter, I'd be up at seven, leaving the cosy caravan for a white blanket of mist that swirled around my ankles as I stomped through the mud to feed the livestock. Michaela would run off just before eight to catch the train to London from Ipswich Station, while Rick and I would start cracking on with producing sausages and bacon to sell at our growing circuit of farmers' markets. We'd have to start our preparations for each market five days beforehand, so we'd be ready on the day with the signs, labels and produce, and the night before we'd hitch up the chiller to the van, ready for the off. When we weren't concentrating on the markets, there was plenty of other work to be done: a farm needs constant maintenance so there were always repairs to do, fences to mend, animals to care for and watch over, and all the day-to-day running of a busy farm. And all that was besides the mountain of paperwork, setting up the farm shop and running the website. . . In fact, I'd find myself wearing the different caps of farmer, butcher, producer, salesman, manager and organiser, often forgetting to eat lunch, until the afternoon turned to dusk and it was time to feed the animals again, just before Michaela made it home around 8pm. I was grateful for the toasty warm caravan at the end of the day, even if I'd never quite managed to get used to the lurid pink interior.

With each day that passed, we seemed to get a little bit closer to getting things sorted and realising our dream. But autumn was nearly over and the days were starting to fade to a much greyer winter.

OPPOSITE Once the trees are bare in autumn, it's a great time to search the woodland floor for the perfect fallen branch to make a walking stick.

WINTER off to market

The winter months on the farm were as hard as they were grey – the glorious hot summer now seemed like a distant memory. The farmer's life is a pleasant if exhausting one when the sun shines; it's just as exhausting but also miserable when the weather is freezing, wet and windy. My first winter on the farm was a tough one, with depressing skies, relentless rain, and wind that shot through the fields of our little exposed peak of Suffolk. But while the skies seemed forever grey, the reality of our situation was black and white. If The Essex Pig Company didn't make money this season, I feared we would lose everything as we spiralled into debt.

As the finances dwindled, we had no choice but to step up yet another gear to make the project work but now we had the elements to battle with as well. Thank goodness for the days when swirls of white mist crept into the woodland, spread over the lower, marshy fields and made the farm feel wonderfully magical, and those rare but bright, crisp, sunny mornings when the refreshing bolt of clear blue sky gave welcome relief from the grey. The pigs had ploughed over all of the grass in the meadow, leaving a boggy mess that the rain turned into a swamp and many of the wild animals in the woodland went into their annual hibernation. As the days grew shorter, we felt an added pressure to get things done before the nights drew in completely.

Back to the market place

There was no time to lose and, with the farm shop not yet open, the quickest and most immediate way of making cash seemed to be selling our produce at farmers' markets. The National Exhibition Centre (NEC) in Birmingham was to hold an enormous food fair and we were determined to turn the five-day event into a cash cow.

Five days! Rick and I had never attended an event of that scale – the duration and the amount of preparation that would be needed sounded gruelling to both of us. We had, after all, got used to spending most of our days in the great outdoors and knew that we would be enclosed in an unnatural world of bright lights and heating, swarming with hundreds of people, including celebrity chefs, for a whole working week; an exciting contrast to the isolation of the farm, but a stark one nonetheless. Five days also meant that we needed one hell of a load of sausages. . . Rick and I spent the week leading up to the fair frantically making a mountain of sausages: Essex Pork, Suffolk Farmhouse, Autumn, Cambridge, Beer, Essex Love and Norfolk Red. We also prepared some streaky bacon and some Saddleback dry-cured bacon for the event. We ordered a ton of labels from Bizerba (our label producer) and more packaging than Father Christmas needs, to keep our products fresh and looking professional. The last thing we wanted was to sell out of sausages and bacon as we had done at the Food Lovers' Fair in Covent Garden. This time we just had to get it right.

The night before the big event, we packed up the chiller van with a huge amount of freshly made sausages, hundreds of shiny rashers of vacuum-packed bacon and, to add a

OPPOSITE **The ginger-coloured Tamworth is a marvellous pig with a lively personality. It will readily make a break for freedom if given half a chance.**

bit of variety, some pheasants and partridges from a local farm, and set off for Birmingham. It was one of those cold, damp, drizzly evenings when the warmth of home beckons and the motorway seems to go on forever – and don't get me started on the infamous Spaghetti Junction. But we finally arrived at the sprawling exhibition centre, unpacked our supplies and put up our tiny stall in the Henrietta Green's Food Lovers' Fair section of the vast event. Our set-up was swift and smooth – it was, by now, a well-rehearsed routine – but we did briefly panic at the fact that the electricity had not yet been turned on. So we did all we could and headed for a neighbouring hotel. As part of our plan to cut costs, we decided to kip on the floor of a friend who had already checked in. Naughty, I know, but five nights for the two of us in the hotel at the fair would have put a huge hole in our takings and we just couldn't afford the luxury of our own private beds and matching en-suites. So we raided a linen cupboard in the hallway for towels, shared out the blankets on the bed and slept on the carpet as best we could.

Bright and early the next morning, we headed out of the hotel door for our first day of the show – and it was crazy. Traders were flapping around and getting ready for the doors opening, workmen were putting the finishing touches to the huge stages and platforms that had been erected for celebrity chefs to hold court, the vast halls were already swarming with activity, and there were we, tucked round a tiny corner in the Food Lovers' Fair section, melting quietly under the bright lights. We were one of about thirty stalls under Henrietta Green's banner, feeling fairly insignificant in the massive sprawl of the trade show, but excited to be part of it nonetheless. We counted down the seconds to the doors opening before the first stampede of people mobbed the halls, just like the first day of the Harrods Sale. The visitors could buy virtually anything to do with food and drink within the halls, from pots and pans to fresh Morecombe Bay fish, sampling just about anything they fancied along the way. And, boy, did everyone make the most of it. The atmosphere was fantastic and so was the camaraderie. Rick and I were happy to see the familiar faces of traders we knew, including our old friend Peter Gott. Many of the people from our regular circuit of farmers' markets were at the fair to do business. It made me feel as though we were circus performers, travelling with the troupe to meet up at the same places to put on a show in the big top. At the end of a hard day's trading at the fair, we often got together for a big curry and a well-deserved pint, making some new friends in the process. That was after we'd had a few samples of wine and whisky from the fair's stalls towards the end of trading each day.

We had hundreds of visitors at The Essex Pig Company stall over those five days, from my mum to Anthony Worrall Thompson but, depressingly, not half as many of the punters put their hands in their pockets as I had hoped. I just couldn't understand it – as far as I could see, we were doing everything right. It felt good to be part of the show, for people to know who we were and what we were doing, but that till just wasn't opening as many times as I'd banked on. At the end of the fair, we made our way home, tired and not quite as chipper as I'd hoped we would be. I reminded myself that nothing was wasted and that we'd still made a decent showing, but it was hard not to feel downhearted – I hadn't figured on the farm not being able to sell as much of its excellent produce as I'd so confidently expected.

As for our regular circuit of farmers' markets, by mid-November we had established ourselves at five per week. Some were a monthly event, others fortnightly and some weekly. You could find The Essex Pig Company on tour, stopping at Braintree, Bedford, Cambridge, Dulwich College in southeast London, Hadleigh in Essex, and the Sainsbury's car park in Norwich, selling our quality sausages and bacon. It was exhausting, prepping the products, making sure the packaging was right, marketing ourselves, setting up the stalls in the winter weather, trading all day in the cold, packing up and then heading back to the farm to a backlog of work. Most market stall holders in their right minds had someone else to do the majority of these tasks, saving themselves for a bit of banter with the punters on the day. But not us. Luckily, I was surrounded by people who would help me out. Rick had perfected the art of butchery beautifully, Asa had the market-trader act down to such a T that you'd think he'd been behind a stall all his life, and Michaela and Lynn helped out with the packaging, pricing and whatever else we needed a hand with, whenever and wherever they could. Before too long, and despite our disappointing NEC experience, we signed up for another big event, the BBC Festive Good Food Show at London's Earl's Court. And this time, I also had lots of assistance from Linda and Meg, two

BELOW The sausages, bacon and joints produced from our pigs always sell well at farmers' markets; once tasted, never forgotten.

ABOVE Feeding time on the farm. During the winter, when there's not much for pigs (or anyone else) to forage, it's essential to give them the nutrients they need to grow big and healthy.

lovely ladies I'd met through Asa. Besides just being pals with Linda and Meg, he sometimes helped out with their Moving Feasts Company. Being caterers, they're real foodies too and were happy to give me a hand on my stall at Earl's Court when I told them that it looked like I might be there on my own. With so much still to do on the farm, Rick really needed to crack on there and couldn't really spare two whole days for the event.

I turned up at the show and unpacked the chiller, a mean task in itself for just one person, but it was well worth the slog. Henrietta Green's Food Lovers' Fair was, among the four hundred plus stands within the Main Hall. There was plenty of Christmas madness, some new ideas for festive cookery as well as the traditional staples, gadgets galore and some of the best local and regional food around, all under one roof that was decked with boughs of holly. To top it off, there were cookery theatres, where celebrity chefs such as Rick Stein, Gordon Ramsay and Jamie Oliver would perform for the crowds.

I was so pleased to see Linda and Meg that morning. They showed up just before we got trading on the first day and they were brilliant. I still found myself running around, talking to customers, working the till, selling sausages and cooking samples, but it was fantastic to have a great team with me to help take the strain. It also meant that in the less busy moments I could take a break, have a browse, do a bit of Christmas shopping and check out the competition. I stocked up on goodies to take home to Mum in Essex. I was particularly keen to find a Three Bird Roast for Christmas day. It's a tradition that goes back to medieval times; the cook would bone a variety of birds, from quails to wood pigeons and pheasants, and carefully stuff them all inside a swan. Today the dish is simpler and, of course, minus the swan as it's a protected bird, but the tradition of removing all the bones, except those in the wing of the goose, remains, so that when you slice through the roast, there is nothing but meat. It tastes amazing, especially if you serve it with a good-quality fruit jelly. I eventually found exactly what I was looking for – an roast of pheasant stuffed into a chicken which was stuffed into a goose. Fantastic! It really put me in the festive spirit.

Back on the stall, I spent quite a bit of my time cooking samples and chatting to the punters, while Linda and Meg helped out with the sales. Everything seemed to be running smoothly when I put one particular batch of sausages on the sizzle. I was chatting away to the customers, turning the sausages slowly as they cooked thinking, 'Strange, these look a bit pink'. They did look really odd but I just couldn't fathom why and I was wondering if the whole batch looked the same. Then, just by chance, Peter Gott popped over from his stand, took one look at the sausages and instantly knew what was going on. Peter figured that Rick must have put salt and saltpetre (usually used in bacon curing) into the sausages instead of sausage seasoning. It's an easy mistake, because the tubs of the stuff look identical. In fact, the reason Peter knew what had happened was because he had once done the same thing himself. Fortunately it wasn't too much of a disaster, it just meant that the bright pink sausages were very, very salty and probably had customers running to the drinks stands having tasted our samples. But poor Rick was devastated when I told him. I was encouraged by our reception at Earl's Court, though. It wasn't as bad as the NEC experience by any means, and it meant that we could be a bit more hopeful about the future.

It was good to spend a few days back on the farm before Christmas. I caught up with paperwork, checked that the animals were doing okay and worked on getting the farm shop ready for its grand opening. I have to admit that the weather seemed to take a lot of the fun out of farming life: the icy winds stung my cheeks so fiercely some days that they shone red with windburn and looked as though they'd been attacked with sandpaper. We seemed to be forever filthy, as the pigs and the rain had turned the fields into a bog and we found ourselves constantly covered in a heady mix of mud and pig shit. Lovely!

Physical work became tough in the cold, but I was determined that we install electrical fencing in the woodland as I planned to put the pigs in there after Christmas, to let the fields recover, give the pigs a life they'd love and see them as I'd imagined when I first clapped eyes on the farm. What's more, as the weather got colder, the pressure was on to get the fencing up before the ground froze solid and made bashing the fence posts in like trying to hammer them into concrete.

As soon as I could, I enlisted the help of Stan and set to work. Stan is a brilliant spark who'd helped us put the electrics in the farm shop and the caravans. He's yet another friend of Asa's and I've never known his first name but his last one was Stanard, so 'Stan' for short seemed to stick. A few months before, I'd bought everything I needed for the job from a pig-equipment auction, including electrical boxes and chargers. On a fresh clear day, we set to work putting the system together so that the pigs could live free-range in the woodland, but couldn't escape. We put in the fencing using the left-over posts we already had as well as the odd tree that had conveniently fallen in the right place. It took me back to the summer when it had been so hot that the ground had become almost solid in the heat and carrying the heavy post-basher and posts around in the soaring temperatures had been murder. I was relieved to be putting in these ones in cooler weather this time around, although the best time to do this kind of work would be spring, when the soil is really soft – but I couldn't wait.

I had chosen to run the line on the mains electricity because batteries would need changing or recharging frequently and solar panels only do the job when the sun shines We spent a long day setting up the whole thing, running cable through the isolators and plugging everything in, ready to go, and it looked very professional when it was done. I could hardly wait to get the pigs in there but the time wasn't quite right yet. I also knew that despite the hefty current in the wires, I would constantly need to walk the line and keep my eye on it. Pigs love nothing more than to escape and, as they're so clever, I had no doubt that they would keep me busy as they found ways to beat the system and break free. Still, I had all that to look forward to – and there was plenty to worry about before that happened.

Christmas home and away

By the time Christmas was drawing near, we were all shattered. The stresses of our financial situation, the accelerated pace of work and the gruelling reality of winter on the farm had taken its toll on everybody. I thought we all deserved a bit of fun so I decided to throw an impromptu Christmas party in the barn to thank everyone for all their hard work. I invited Dolly, Matt, Stan the electrician, some of the local farmers who had helped out, such as Ben and Russell from the neighbouring farm, as well as Rick, Lynn and the kids. I rushed around that day, making tables out of straw bales and fridge panels, sweeping down the barn, organising a heater and music, as well as putting up fairy lights. Then I cooked us a bit of a feast on the rickety old cooker we had inherited with the farm that stood at the back of the barn. Despite its low-tech options of 'hot or not', I still managed to serve belly of pork with leeks and a rustic mash peppered with chunks of carrots for all. Terrific! It was a great night. We all kicked back, released our tensions and enjoyed the spirit of the season over whisky macs (whisky and green ginger wine) followed by a glass of wine or two with dinner. Cosy indoors, we enjoyed a few laughs, built up morale and talked about the little things that had been niggling us as the icy air whipped round the

ABOVE As long as pigs have decent shelter and comfy straw to bed down in at night, they are happy to be outside in most weathers. Their layers of fat and their bristly coats keep them warm even in the depths of winter.

barn outside. It was a wonderfully festive occasion that felt like a traditional farm Christmas party and gave me the chance to say my thank yous to everyone before I shot off for Christmas. I was pretty excited about my plans: first it was a trip to my family home in Essex for Christmas and then – Australia!

It might have seemed a bad time to cough up for the price of trip down under but in fact it had all been arranged long before I'd even started my project on the farm. My good friends Matt (a sommelier at Jamie's restaurant) and his girlfriend Carly had decided a while ago to get married in Melbourne at Christmas and Michaela and I had booked to go to the wedding. There was no way I could pull out now and, actually, I was now glad that I was going. I knew that it would be good for me to take a break from the farm: it had been all I'd thought about and worked for over the last eight months and I needed to clear my head and get a bit of perspective. It would also be just as important for Rick to run the farm on his own – it would be brilliant for his confidence and he was keen to show me that he could do it. So, all in all, I was dead chuffed as I packed my bags, dusted down my suit and dug out my 'sunnies', as they say in Oz.

As Michaela headed off to her mum's in France for Christmas, I drove to Essex, with the Three Bird Roast of pheasant, chicken and goose that I'd bought at Earl's Court, and a load of pressies for the family. Christmas Day was lovely and I relished the comfort of being back at home, enjoying the familiar festive rituals and taking a break from running around like a madman, adapting to whatever was thrown at me on the farm. We had a good old-fashioned Christmas meal and drinks on the big day, with the whole family including my aunt and uncle, and then we all crashed out on Boxing Day which was really great.

The day after that I found myself on a twenty-four-hour flight to Melbourne, feeling slightly surreal as I saw the land disappear after take-off and heard the hum of the engine replace the animal noises I was so used to on the farm. Despite the long flight, I was still extremely excited to set foot in Australia, with the blazing sunshine a complete opposite to the greyness of home. Melbourne was fantastic. Michaela flew out to meet me and, along with three friends also attending the nuptials, we stayed bang on the coast. It was a real novelty to go out for meals in the evening in the wonderful light and warmth, knowing it was gloomy on the farm and that someone else was worrying about the animals and trudging about looking after them. Although I had the greatest intentions of doing research into Australian farming, my plans didn't actually come too much. I thought I would take a trip down to Port Campbell, a good day's drive out of town, heading west along the Great Ocean Road, to check out some Wessex pigs (as opposed to Essex pigs), and I was curious to learn about farming on this side of the world. But as soon as I stopped work I found that I was just too exhausted to travel around. I did, however, manage to visit some markets and taste the local produce, including Australian bacon, which is completely different to ours. And I learnt that Australia has the perfect environment for making cheese, although there is not much cheese production going on there. But I spent the majority of the time trying not to think too hard about work, enjoying my friends' wedding and re-charging my batteries for what I knew would be a full-on return.

Meanwhile, Rick and his family had a great Christmas on the farm. For a really traditional Christmas lunch, they had killed and cooked the first goose any of us had eaten from our stock and served it with a potato stuffing and all of the trimmings (see page 200 for the recipe). They had also bought a live turkey to kill and eat over the festive period, although their plan was scuppered. It only lasted a week on the farm before a fox got there first. But Christmas on the farm hadn't all been about fun and holidays. Rick had worked hard, taking some pigs to slaughter, trading single-handed at a couple of farmers' markets, and feeding the animals every day – all mammoth tasks for just one person.

I had had an amazing break in Australia but towards the end of our holiday, I was keen to get back to the farm and get my teeth into the next phase of the project. The day we arrived back put me in a fighting mood, too. After what seemed to be a never-ending flight from Melbourne, my friends Simon and Haley and I landed at 5am on a cold London morning. Hungry, we stopped for breakfast at a service station on the motorway heading home to Suffolk, where we looked forward to British eggs and bacon. But when our breakfast came, we were served an inedible fry-up on a plate swimming in grease and

OPPOSITE Pigs love grubbing about in the earth but make an awful mess of it, so it's important to move them from field to field. This provides them with fresh earth to forage and allows the depleted area to recover.

piled with horrible battery eggs, watery bacon, rubbish fried bread and a price tag of £9.80. I wouldn't have minded paying for a decent breakfast with lovely chunky rustic sausages, fresh free-range eggs and a lovely toasted country loaf – but with jet lag, an empty stomach and an abomination on a plate in front of me, I lost the plot. I ended up having a huge row with the manager, trying to get him to justify his mark up on the rubbish he was serving. I was fuming but, at the same time, it got me right back into what I was trying to do on the farm. I found myself racing back to Suffolk to crack on with our quality food production and get straight back on track.

I remember turning up to the farm that morning. It was a bitter, mean day with dark skies that seemed almost black in contrast to the sunny blue of Melbourne, but it was great to see everyone again. I loved catching up with the news, hearing how their Christmases had been, and checking on all of the animals after being away. The pigs, sheep, ducks and geese all seemed fine, but I couldn't believe it when I set eyes on Cora. My tearaway terrier had been up to her usual tricks while I'd been away and this time she'd got caught out. Cora and Parker had run off to chase rabbits, as they often did, but they'd strayed away from the farm and old Cora had obviously paid more attention to finding warrens than to on-coming traffic. After the dogs had been out of sight for hours, Rick had gone to look for them and found Cora lying at the side of a country lane, with

BELOW Farming is a demanding occupation all year round, but it's especially tough during the winter, when you have to do all the usual tasks in sub-zero temperatures.

Parker lying on top of her to keep her warm. She had been hit by a car. Lynn had rushed her off to the vet and now she was a sorry sight, hobbling around with one leg in what looked like a dog-sized welly boot that held her broken limb together and encouraged it to heal. It was such a shame to see her like this – the old girl looked really sorry for herself and seemed to have lost all of her spark, but of course I was just relieved that she was still with us. I felt a bit sorry for Rick, too – he had done a brilliant job of looking after things on the farm, but he felt as though something went wrong when I went away and he took it personally. It hadn't helped that a fox had got into the chicken house one night and had swiped our Maran cockerel and a few of our chickens, including a Light Sussex hen and some of the rarer breeds. Now the fox knew that there was a good supply of tasty birds on the farm, we all knew he would be back time after time. We planned to ask our neighbours Ben and Russell to stake it out one night and shoot it if they could.

The new year arrives

Once I'd been back from Australia for a few days, it felt as though I'd never been away. The weather took a turn for the worse and we had our first snow flurries on the farm. One January morning, we woke up to see the place looking wonderful, all crisp and whiter than white. The snow hid the rusty old pipes, the lost tiles and all of the imperfections on the farm and made it appear pristine. From my steamy caravan window, I could see Woody and Jade had run out to play. I've never seen Jade so excited and Woody, who had never seen snow before, just went bonkers. He ran around in circles, pounced on the snow with all four paws as if it would all suddenly move once it had settled on the ground and tried to catch it as it fell from the billowing sky. But snow on a farm is never good news for a farmer and the novelty soon wore off. I went to turn on a tap to make my first cuppa of the day and found that the pipes were frozen solid. So out we went, sorely missing our breakfast, to make sure the animals were warm enough. We trundled through the snow with straw bales, spreading them around with our pitchforks to make a bed for each of the animals, to make sure they were comfortable. It sounds like a simple task but it was a harsh five hours of to-ing and fro-ing as the snow continued to fall. Our hats flew off in the wind, we were frozen to the bone and a number of times I would try and open a gate with one hand, holding a straw bale with the other, only to have it slam shut on me again, much to the sheep's annoyance. But farm life has taught me that these tasks can't be rushed – I had to adopt a slower pace of life, because trying to do things quickly would have meant a whole farce of slamming gates and twitchy animals that refused to be moved in a hurry.

One small sow had just had a litter; both she and her piglets were tiny and there wasn't much milk in the old girl. As we approached them in the snow, I could see the little chaps quivering with cold in the icy wind so we took the decision to take the piglets and their mum out of the field and put them into the barn. We found a cosy corner, made a bed for them to curl up in and hoped it would bring the little ones on a bit. At least in the barn they could get their trotters warm again. We also put Jasper in with the youngsters. He had been doing well, but we didn't want to take any chances. Once all of the animals were warm, we set about feeding them before trying to get our water flowing again. Since the summer we'd got used to the luxury of hot water on tap and it was frustrating not be able to take a shower, but we had no choice other than to wait until the pipes defrosted and pray they didn't burst. We went through the same routine for the next two days as the snow continued to fall. And eventually, on the third morning the weather lifted and the rain came, turning everything to slush and mud.

For a while now, Asa had been living with us. It was great to have him around because we always had a laugh and he was brilliant at helping out, but the caravan had become spatially challenged for three adults and three dogs. So Asa made the decision to buy his own mobile home and live on-site. He had always loved spending time on the farm, ever since the very first days, and his plan was to work with us and help us trade at the farmers' markets, and take the odd local security job when he fancied. He saw it as an opportunity to get fit again, live more of a healthy, outdoor life and have space to relax when he wasn't working. Before long he had his own caravan delivered to the back field, had painted all of the walls, fitted a carpet and got it half decorated before moving in. As soon as he did, he started working properly with The Essex Pig Company. Apart from helping out with the day-to-day running of the farm, we had already discovered that Asa was absolutely brilliant at markets, charming the punters and coaxing them to buy with his superb patter. Now he started learning butchery with Rick and, in no time at all, he was making his own sausages and bacon as well as building up a clientele at the farmers' markets. All good stuff. But maybe his biggest achievement was personal. The change in lifestyle, diet and fresh air as well as a new routine of running and boxing with his punch bag in the barn, meant that Asa lost a whopping three stone in three months. He could have marketed that diet to rival Atkins. I remember one night in particular we realised how trim the chap had become when he was on his way back to Bury St Edmunds for a drink with some of his old mates. While he was getting ready, Asa discovered that none of his old clothes seemed to fit him. Waddling over to my caravan, he looked hilarious in trousers belted up round his armpits so that they stayed up, transforming them into grandad's trousers, and we all rolled around laughing. I just had to lend him one of my suits. He never dreamed that it would fit, but it was perfect and Asa went out looking as sharp as James Bond and three stone lighter. His friends all did a double-take when he walked into the pub that night: they weren't expecting his new physique, never mind someone who worked on a farm to look so good.

Sadly, in the winter weather, not everything was running as slickly as Asa. It was a season beset with power cuts and it wasn't unusual for our whole system to short-circuit.

OPPOSITE Here is one of our fine British Lops enjoying a rather muddy forage in one of the fields.

Admittedly, sometimes we overloaded the system ourselves as we simultaneously tried to boil a kettle, have the lights blaring, use the equipment to make sausages and take a shower in a caravan. But, more often than not, a bit of snow or a fierce gale was enough to knock the power off. And we'd be there, all wet and muddy at 9pm, wanting a shower and trying to cook an evening meal, having to rummage around for a torch to the sound of whatever we had simmering on the hob sizzling out and turning cold. At times like those, there was nothing to do but pull on a clean pair of jeans and trainers and head for the pub.

Of course, there were far worse things that happened than the power cuts that tested our patience. Sadly, that January, there was a death on the farm. Early one morning, I noticed that one of the female Saddlebacks had developed a nasty cough. I'd learnt how to administer an injection against pneumonia when I'd visited Peter's farm so we moved the pig into the barn to make her warm and comfortable, and gave her the shot, but she died in the night. It was pretty awful to discover her the next morning, lying stiff and heavy in the barn, and I was sad that we hadn't managed to save her. Some pigs respond well to antibiotics and I'd learnt that if we caught a chill early enough they can pick up pretty quickly – but not this time. Maybe it was too little too late but, as the vet said, where you have livestock you have dead stock. It was just another reality of farming life.

When the bone man turned up that afternoon on his weekly round, I had a little more for him than the odd pig head and usual debris from sausage-making. The bone

BELOW Although we lost one pig to respiratory problems, we got through the winter largely unscathed and with high hopes for the future. We lived by the rule – cold winters call for warm housing – so our stock was protected during the harsh months.

man is the official collector of dead stock. What a terrible job! But somehow our chap manages to stay jolly as he turns up in his big, white, reeking truck with its large dark bins on the back. I don't know how he keeps his sense of humour, but I can only guess it gets him through the day. I can't help wondering how he explains what he does when he's down the pub – it must be a bit like introducing yourself as the grim reaper.

With incidents like these during the bleak winter months, we faced up to taking the rough with the smooth on the farm. Our financial situation was no exception: at possibly the darkest point of the season, I discovered that we had run up a deficit of around £30,000. It was a huge amount of money but it had built up gradually and with good reason. We'd forked out for pig feed, fuel, plumbers, electricians, building materials, wages, fencing and insurance, and our business plan had optimistically banked on the farm shop being up and running by September, almost five months earlier. It wasn't as though I had been taking any money from the profits we made at the farmers' markets – in fact, I had been hoping to be able to start paying myself a small salary of, say, £100 a week by this point in the plan, but any profit now had to go towards paying off the deficit. It was a constant worry and loomed over us constantly, but I was determined it wouldn't beat us.

Our financial problems were just another pressure on a long list of stresses of running a farm and, when I sat down to think about it, I wondered how I hadn't gone crackers. By the winter, I had built and more or less set up the farm shop, helped repair some of the outbuildings, been a stall holder, a producer, a marketing and PR man as well as a farmer. I sometimes had to walk into a cupboard to scream and try and get it all into perspective. And, just like the bone man, I had to hang on to my sense of humour. I remember one day Michaela and I were having a huge row in the caravan, ranting and raving at each other in the lounge for a reason I can't recall. I rushed into the bedroom to get out of the way, slammed the door in a fit of fury, and the light fitting came loose and nearly knocked me out as it fell on my head. You have to laugh, though – what else can you do? Most importantly, I had to hold on to why I was doing all of this. It had never been for the money, but for a better quality of life in the countryside and putting into practice a lot of things I had come to believe in about animal welfare and food production. On that basis, I had, in fact, fulfilled many of my personal goals and they weren't about a load of numbers on a piece of paper. When I thought of it that way, it helped to make things seem less drastic.

The farm shop evolves. . .

The farm shop would be fundamental to the survival of the farm and we were still focused on getting it up and open to the public as soon as possible. We had been searching for furniture to add warmth and country charm to the clinical white box of the shop, but we hadn't had much luck with the free ads and the Internet, so Asa and I decided that an auction was the only way to go. Michaela, Asa and I set off to Websters the local auction house, one wintry morning to bag ourselves some bargains. Having done our homework, we knew that a great Welsh dresser with a reserve of £200 was due to come up that day, along with other lots that included a pine farmhouse table, some great chairs that would work with it, and a rug. Perfect!

It was a busy day at the auction and the seats were packed with a mix of professional dealers and people like us, looking to find a bit of treasure or take something home at a snip of its real value. There were also a few farmers there, ready to tip their flat caps, but I had a secret weapon – our market trader Asa, who definitely had the gift of the gab. He was ready and focused, which is more than I can say for myself. Michaela insisted on coming as she had her heart set on the dresser and she kept reining me in as I got distracted and bought tools and pieces of farming equipment. Nevertheless, Asa and I managed to beat off the competition to get the farmhouse table for £45. Then, as we got into the spirit of things, I got a phone call on my mobile to say some pigs had jumped the fence. I decided to leave Asa to work his magic, assisted by

BELOW An interesting addition to the farm was the wild boar/Tamworth cross, who was rather a character.

Michaela, as I shot off to round up the little porkers. And I am glad that I did. At the first opportunity of a tea break, Asa loudly announced that he was looking forward to the dresser coming up. He made sure that everyone could hear him say that he was prepared to bid all day for it and would pay whatever it took. So, as proceedings got under way and the dresser was wheeled out with its reserve of £200, Asa clinched the deal for just £210 amid an audience who probably assumed they'd lost it before the bidding had begun.

Asa and Michaela brought the furniture back to the farm in the van, including the rug which they'd also managed to secure at a bargain-basement price, and we all got excited about transforming the shop. But it took a ton of work and a big team effort before it finally came together.

In the weeks that ran up to the opening, we planned and plotted our every move like a military operation to make sure the shop finally opened and didn't disappoint. We got the furniture swiftly into place and couldn't wait to dress the shop. Our aim was to keep the side where the butchery took place completely clean and hygienic with no frills, while the shop would feel more like walking into a country kitchen with a fantastic pantry, much more homely than your average shop. We wanted to evoke a rustic charm and create an atmosphere that was inviting and comfortable, so we spent time perfecting the lighting and decorating the walls with some great pictures of pigs and other art that was for sale. We organised the fridges ready for produce, dusted down some wicker baskets I had collected that would display jams, tea, coffee and other dry foods, and bought some dried flowers from Brandon's nursery along the road to liven up the place. We also decided to sell books on nature and wildlife. But that was just the beginning of our preparations.

As part of my plan to make quality food accessible, we had set up our mail order and online businesses. I couldn't expect people to travel to the Suffolk countryside for our produce. Our website allowed people to shop at home and receive a nice little parcel through the post, this brought the tradition of farming bang up to date with the help of technology. I loved the idea of the fusion although I can't pretend that it was my own. I'd met one of my friend's dads, a guy called Andy Sebire, who breeds traditional Hereford cows at his farm called Lower Hurst. He sells the most fantastic beef online and when I first ordered and tasted it, I couldn't decide which was more impressive – the mouth-watering joint in front of me, or the brilliant way in which it had arrived. From then on, I considered the worldwide web essential to the modern farming business. Trouble is, I am a bit of a technophobe, but as I said before with the help of my cousin Amy the site was soon up and running.

I only hoped that the shop opening would run more smoothly than the first website orders I handled as The Essex Pig Company. When I received my first two requests by e-mail for our products, I had to blink hard and read them twice, I was so excited. I ordered some special boxes so that the orders would arrive in pristine condition, filled one with our hand-made sausages and the other with our home-cured bacon, wrapped the parcels up very carefully and sent them off. I didn't expect to hear from the same customers again for a while at least, but I picked up two phone calls from them immediately – result! The orders had arrived the very next day, which impressed the punters no end, they told me in chipper tones, but the lady who had wanted sausages had unfortunately received bacon, and the gentleman who had ordered the bacon was sent sausages.

Meanwhile, as I waited for more orders to hit my inbox, we decided to make the day of the grand opening a really big event. Not only would we open the doors to customers for the first time, we would also host our first farmers' market on the farm. There would be gas heaters in the barn, with a row of stalls down each side, spilling outside on to a fresh layer of newly laid gravel in front of the shop. It was a great idea that would add colour and interest to the shop opening, so we spent some of our time at the markets we attended scouting out the finest stalls and asking them if they would like to trade at our farm on the big day. We called other producers from the surrounding areas and invited them to come, and soon found that we were taking bookings, from two weeks in advance right up to two days before the event. We secured a fantastic mix of food stands, selling everything from freshly made bread, cottage-style cakes, spicy chutneys, fruity jams and hot soup, as well as Morecombe Bay potted shrimp, smoked salmon and locally grown fruit and veg. It made my mouth water just thinking about it.

Then we faced up to the testing task of marketing our own event. I knew the fact that Jamie had agreed to open the shop with me would help get people there, so we produced hundreds of leaflets with Jamie's name on, a map our arty neighbours had drawn for us and details of the farm shop opening. We then set about distributing them far and wide, handing them out furiously at farmers' markets, down the pub and in Ipswich city centre. At one point we even started carrying them wherever we went, but we often returned with almost as many and it became soul-destroying – people often just walked passed us without any acknowledgement. In the end, perseverance prevailed and we managed to hand out the majority of our leaflets. Finally, we almost had everything in place for the big day.

And then there were goats. . .

There were quite a lot of other events happening on the farm while we were preparing for the big opening. Aside from our daily duties of looking after and feeding the animals, we were shifting some of them around, accumulating more in the process and being accredited for our rare breed meats.

Rick had an idea that it would be great to have a few goats on the farm for when kids pulled up to the farm shop with their mums and dads. Having seen how much goats seem to amuse little ones, I agreed. Besides, I knew that goats are hardy and fairly low maintenance, needing only scrubby pasture to graze on. In fact, I had read that they were able to survive on very little when kept in mountainous or desert conditions, but I didn't know that the inherent hardy and unfussy nature that makes them so easy to look after also means that they are troublesome, stubborn blighters too.

As with most animals, including pigs, goats like to be kept in pairs at least. Before long, Rick found us three crosses, a mother and her two daughters, to give a home to on the farm. Rick bought the goats from a lady called Mrs Jones after Animal Mark spotted her ad offering them for sale, and he brought them back in the trailer to their new home. But when he opened the trailer to put them in the front field, they just didn't seem to want to come out at all. We thought maybe they were a bit wary of somewhere new and that maybe they were a bit disorientated by the journey, so we treated them carefully, in case they were nervous. It took a while but we gently coaxed the goats out and let them go. Almost immediately our sheep came rushing over to see what was going on and the goats bolted, charging off, at top speed. I was on my mobile to the vet at the time as I watched the goats dash round the back of the farm, hop one fence and then hop another fence with more ease than your average hurdler and disappear into the countryside.

BELOW We introduced goats to the farm mainly for the benefit of children visiting the farm shop with their parents. It took tremendous patience on our part to get the goats to settle down, but once they did, they were a great draw.

Tips on Keeping Goats

• Goats are popular with smallholders because they are pretty low maintenance. They can supply you with fantastic milk and cheese for relatively little trouble, as they are naturally healthy animals. If you don't have a lot of land but would like to keep a dairy animal, they're ideal. And if you can put up with their antics, they're also great fun.

• Despite their hardiness goats do not like rain, cold or damp weather, so you need to provide them with some draught-free shelter in the winter months and at night. A barn or large shed is ideal. Goats like a pile of straw for bedding and that keeps them warmer in the winter months. I suggest you opt for a sturdy door, so that they don't escape.

• Even more than pigs, goats eat everything in sight – useful should you want to get rid of a stubborn patch of weeds, which they prefer to grass. This also means that you can keep your goats on a part of your land that's not so popular with the other animals. But be warned: their love of outdoor nibbling won't always work in your favour. Watch out for your hedges – to a goat, they're a tasty meal, not a boundary – as well as your flowers and herbs. Goats will eat bushes, shrubs and strip the bark from trees, not just eating but killing most things green.

• Although goats are happiest when eating what comes naturally outdoors, they will need their natural diet supplemented with hay and rolled oats. This is important,

especially if you want them to produce milk. Hay provides goats with the roughage they need and I would recommend that you give it to them morning and evening, or invest in a hay rack (a wire slatted box that you can put in the goat house for regular nibbling). You can buy ready-mixed cereal rations, called concentrates, to give your goats daily, which will include all of the nutrients and minerals they need. Alternatively you could make up your own mix of rolled oats, bran, linseed flakes, dry sugar-beet pulp or kibbled beans in equal parts, although you will probably find it more expensive to do so.

• Goats need salt licks – they look like giant bars of soap and contain the minerals essential for health.

• As with pigs, goats are boisterous at feeding time and will often knock over buckets or troughs. Either weigh or tie down your feeders, or, if you are keeping just two or three goats, you could put large bowls down and remove them when the goats have cleared them. You will also need to ensure that goats have a constant and plentiful supply of water, but secure your buckets or they'll be forever knocking them over.

• Finally, a word – I suggest that you invest in very high fencing if you're keeping goats! But don't expect them not to jump or eat right through it. If you choose to tether them, you must move them around regularly, for their own interest and to keep them free of internal parasites.

It was late in the evening and luckily the goats didn't go far. We soon found that two of them had ended up at a neighbour's farm – the stable girl spotted them, stood her ground as they charged towards her, and shut the two of them in an empty horse stable so that we could come and drag them back home. Goodness knows where the other one ran off to but she soon reappeared on our farm, although I couldn't catch her for love nor money. Now that Rick had the other goats back on our land, I tied a long rope around the old girl when she was distracted on seeing her daughters and walked her out so the other goats could see her too. My plan soon worked and the other goats started to follow us. I walked the goat like a dog into the barn and hid, signalling to Rick to shut the door when we and the three goats were all in there. Sounds simple enough but this was only a theory. It took about five attempts for us to get it right and in the meantime our blunders were like extracts from one of those out-take shows. The first time, I knocked over a straw bale I was hiding behind and the goats ran out of the barn door, spooked. The second time, Rick couldn't shut the door in time and the goats slipped past him. On the third go, one goat knocked over a bucket and startled the others. And on the fourth, a whole string of calamities had us roaring, which of course made the goats jumpy again. We finally ended up with all three goats in the barn – but how would we ever get them to live outside and not run off?

I was learning that goats are very, very clever; they are quick and intelligent, especially when it comes to hatching escape plans. To begin with, we put dog collars on them and tied them all to tractor tyres so that they could get out of the barn and over to the field for the day, but not run off. We thought we'd cracked it. The first goat ran out, pulled the rope until it was taut and then stayed where she was. No problem. The other goats followed but managed to snap their collars free and bolted, yet again. Rick and I were fast becoming world champion rugby tacklers. Eventually we had to get the goats proper chains and collars so that we could let them out every day, tie them up and then take them back in again in the evening. I hated seeing animals restrained in this way, but we had no choice – we just didn't have the time to keep running after them.

From the moment they arrived on the farm, the goats and the sheep seemed to make each other jumpy. But after a few days grazing in the same field, they started to rub along and we decided to cut the goats' chains. Now they wander where they want and go back to the barn to sleep every night. But when I say where they want, that is exactly what I mean: when the farm shop is empty, they hop over the barbed fence with a glint in their eyes, eat the leaves off the trees and any flowerheads from the pots before jumping back home with a fuller stomach. Talk about the life of Riley – they seem to do whatever they please and eat just everything in sight. Maybe it's this sense of anarchy in their personalities that kids love about them. Rick seems to feel a bit bad about suggesting we buy the goats, probably because I'm always moaning that they are extra work, swearing at them, or saying they would make a good curry – but actually I think they're a good thing. Goats are great livestock to keep on a smallholding.

Pigs in the wood

As our goats settled down, I was keen to get the pigs into the woodland before the farm shop opened. For the time being, we'd already moved the pigs from the field to prevent them from completely destroying it and temporarily held them in the courtyard. It was muddy and bleak out there and I couldn't wait to load up the first few pigs on to the trailer and show them their new home. We chose just one of the placid old Tamworths and two Saddlebacks to start off with, as we hadn't yet tested the electrical fence. The best way to check it was all in order was to find out for ourselves by touching it, so Asa, an ex-Royal Marine, and I, the hardy farmer, stood about daring each other to be the first, saying, 'You touch it' and 'No, you touch it' as though we were bantering in the playground. I'm embarrassed to admit that neither of us would go first and after about ten minutes, Stan the spark, who'd installed the fence and had come back to make sure all was well, got tired of both of us, rolled his eyes and reached out his arm. He touched the wire and said he was getting huge shocks from the system but he didn't flinch, so we just didn't believe him. We stood there, disbelieving and insisting he did it again, when Bracken, my spaniel cross, bounded over, skidded a bit in the mud and bumped into the fencing; the poor thing shuddered as a huge shock zapped through her body and we felt terrible. But we knew for sure now that the fence was working so we let the pigs out of

OPPOSITE Pigs are inquisitive creatures, always rooting round for new finds, or following people to see what they're up to. One glimpse of my orange bucket and they know that food is in the offing.

the trailer into their new home – and they went berserk. The Tamworth ran into the woodland with the speed of a new piglet, kicked her legs high into the air and let out the loudest fart I had ever heard (and believe me, pigs often fart very loudly), she was so happy. We moved all of the pigs over in groups and they took to their new environment immediately, snorting and trundling among the trees. They seemed to be more lively than usual, often breaking into a trot, their lopping ears flapping as they bounced, until they stopped dead in their tracks to forage on a new bit of earth. They were in pig heaven. But pigs are pigs which meant that, even though they loved their home, they were continually trying to escape.

We soon discovered that the pigs were even more intelligent than we'd thought and we would often spot several Saddlebacks or Tamworths on a neighbouring field in the distance and have to run off after them. But it was how they executed their escape plans that never ceased to amaze me: they would shunt large branches or logs on to the line with their snouts to short-circuit the fencing electricity supply or pile up mounds of earth on top of the line to do the trick. However many times we brought them back home, they would do it all over again. It was like a piggy remake of *The Great Escape*, which sounds amusing, but for us it wasn't much fun. Getting the pigs back into the woodland could take anything up to three or four hours, a good chunk of a day, and then we would have to try and build up the fencing again, patch up the wire and mend posts, always knowing that despite our best efforts it was an on-going battle.

Of course, we had to be careful of the electric fencing too – one wet afternoon, I was chatting away to Asa, waving my arms around to illustrate a point and not really looking at what I was doing. As we trudged through the muddy field in the pouring rain, I touched the metal gate on the side of the electric fence by mistake. A massive electric shock went from the gate, up one arm, climbed right across my chest, and down the other side. I could feel the line of electricity run through my body as I jerked around doing some involuntary body popping. I was actually smoking! And all Asa could do was bend double in hysterics. Thanks, buddy!

All the trouble was worth it when we saw how brilliantly my plan had worked, and how much the pigs adored their life in the outdoors, following their natural instincts and spending their days the way they were meant to.

The grand opening arrives at last

As the shop neared being ready for business, we prepared for two final inspections of our premises. The first was by the Environmental Health Officer, who had to pass the shop in order for us to trade. I'd already waded through a ton of paperwork in preparation, including one for Hazard Analysis and Critical Control Points which, in plain English, meant writing down a list of possible accidents that could occur while we prepared bacon or made sausages or whatever. We'd already had our fridges and general workspaces tested when the shop was used as a processing plant but they had to be checked again before we were up and running as a shop. I was really nervous when the officer visited – it reminded me of university and having to take a major exam, but there was far more riding on this one. After we'd arranged the visit and knew roughly when the inspection would happen, we swung into Operation Clean-up. But I needn't have worried as, when the day came, my fears were allayed. The inspector turned up in her head-to-toe whites and she was friendly, encouraging and helpful. A lot of people are of the opinion that Environmental Health Officers are nasty people who come along to catch you out, but Emma Richbell, our assigned officer, was fantastic. She was impressed with the quality of our work and we received a health mark. The only minor disaster was that I had unplugged one of our chillers to use the socket do some labelling the morning Emma arrived and had forgotten to plug it back in. She turned up just as it had started to defrost – but Emma took it in her stride once she had checked that everything was OK. I realised that she probably expected these sorts of occurrences as part of the running of a business like ours. Emma made some suggestions and wrote to us to confirm them in writing and as soon as we implemented the changes (such as mending a doddery freezer and having the required amount of hand basins), we got the green light to open the shop.

Our second inspection was even more exciting. We had the Rare Breed Survival Trust (RBST) come to visit. As the name suggests, the trust is a charity founded to ensure that indigenous rare breeds of livestock continue to survive in the UK. Under it's banner,

BELOW Our pigs spent the winter out in the fields, but as the weather gradually improved, we moved them into the woodland, which they absolutely adore.

the trust covers every kind of farmyard animal, from Suffolk Punch horses to Ixworth chickens, and as part of their conservation measures, they also have a fantastic meat-marketing scheme. This not only saves the meat breeds from decline and celebrates and markets their higher eating and health-giving qualities than commercially bred breeds, but also accredits producers whose welfare standards are high and whose breeds are totally traceable. It's a great honour to receive an accreditation.

Naturally I was looking forward to our inspection and hoped that it would result in The Essex Pig Company receiving an accreditation and becoming a member of the RBST meat-marketing scheme. A man called Richard Lutchworth came up to visit the farm, check out our pigs, look at what we would be selling in the farm shop and sample our products. He was happy that our rare-breed meat was of a high standard and quality and I was all smiles as he left me with a huge lever-arch folder of information and a plaque to put in the shop as a badge of honour. Being part of the scheme also meant that I was able to contact farmers of rare breeds that we didn't keep ourselves and access their meat to sell in the shop. I was keen on this idea to give consumers a change and a constant variety and also hoped it would prove to be a bit of an education. I loved the idea that a punter can say, 'We had Dexter beef or a Norfolk Horn roasting joint last night'. They might taste the difference between meats, learn about the food and all the while, ensure the breeds survive. The only downside for me was that it meant a load more form-filling and a levy to the RBST every time I fancied selling something new or different in the shop – but I was getting used to that.

A few days before the shop opening, all of our hard work seemed to come together. Michaela's mum flew in from France to help price up the goods, which ranged from our own farm-fresh eggs to locally dried herbs, and brought some wonderful paintings of farmyard animals to hang and sell on behalf of a friend back in France. Along with my artistic cousin Amy and Michaela's friend Anna, the girls made the place look great. They chalked up the blackboards with prices and descriptions of sausages and bacon and focused on the finishing touches, such as hanging fairy lights in the otherwise stark toilets. We orchestrated our final leaflet drop, slipping hundreds of them under windscreen wipers in Sainsbury's car park. Then, the day before the shop opened, Rick, Asa and I got stuck into making a mountain of sausages, slicing bacon and preparing the fresh joints. In the evening, we gave a warm welcome to friends who had popped down to help out the next day, such as my mates Simon Day and Andy the gas man, but were careful to catch an early night. We knew we would need the rest.

On the morning of the grand opening, we got up ridiculously early but not without good reason. We lads were on a mission to scatter signs around the surrounding countryside so that people could find the farm, and it's not strictly permitted. We set off in the van and jumped out to pin our big fluorescent signs to the odd traffic light,

OPPOSITE **It was a proud moment when the Rare Breed Survival Trust inspected our animals and declared them good enough to be accredited. The sign they awarded us, a guarantee of high quality, hangs outside our farm shop for all to see.**

TRADITIONAL BREEDS

R B S T

MEAT MARKETING~

Accredited Butcher

ABOVE A monumental group effort went into preparing the farm shop for its opening day. Inside it was mixture of clinical hygiene and rustic charm, while outside it was a floral spectacular. We hoped the customers would find it irresistible.

roundabout and gate post at strategic points. Then I convinced Andy and Rick's son Carl to dress up in matching chicken costumes I'd hired so that they could attract some passing trade and direct the traffic down to the farm from the top of the lane. What mates! They stood in their superhero-style yellow tights with their orange chicken's feet, bright orange shorts, nylon yellow body suits and chicken heads for the rest of the morning, It was definitely a frosty one, but the skies were blue and the sun was shining, to everybody's relief.

I was a bit worried about how many people would turn out that day; there was a small local farmers' market on that morning as well as one of the best food fairs in the county run by Taste of Anglia, with some of the excellent suppliers around East Anglia trading there. It would be a big draw to customers and was serious competition. Just my luck, I thought. I had chosen the date of our opening to fit in with Jamie's schedule. But by 9am, cars were arriving as we were still sweeping up and, to my surprise, there were plenty of them – and there was still over an hour to go before the shop officially opened. I'm not sure why but I started to wish that I wasn't on the farm that day. It was a weird feeling. I knew at that point that it would be great, a real achievement and all that we had been working towards, but that it would also be very, very hectic and I wouldn't be able to switch my brain off for a second. At least we were well prepared. I had asked a couple of mates to direct the traffic to park on the top field and cordoned it off with tape. It seemed like the best idea but I hadn't counted on the ground being so boggy from the rain the night before and people were doing wheel spins, getting stuck in the mud and causing a jam. In the end we had to get a neighbour and fellow farmer, Russell, to dig a new entrance for us. Apart from that there were very few hiccups.

As customers, friends, family and press arrived, they parked up and walked the pathway from the field to the farm shop. To do so, they had to walk past the pigs in the woodland, who all gathered around the perimeter of the fencing to trundle alongside, nosy as always. Up and down they went, keen to walk, grunt and look up at all the new faces. The pigs and the punters loved it. From the front of the shop, people could wander into the barn to the farmers' market, visit the stalls that spilled on to the gravel outside and, of course, check out our new shop.

Inside, our produce was beautifully displayed. Michaela and her friends were there to help out in their Essex Pig Company T-shirts; Lynn and my good friend Simon Day were behind the counter; Asa was helping out at every turn and so was Rick, despite a stinking cold and a face like death. Then there were Jules and Sharpie, selling jewel-like jars of their jams and jellies and handing out tastings. For ladies who look sophisticated and glamorous, they're quite crackers and really good fun. I met them through a friend of mine, Louise, and they also sell on Peter's stall sometimes, when he gives them a pitch. I'm not surprised that he does: their homemade chilli jams are wonderful. In fact, they've won a fair few gold awards and have a brilliant reputation within the industry. My personal favourites are their fantastic mint chilli sauce that's great with lamb and a delicious cranberry sauce with a mean chilli kick. There were tons of lovely things to look at and buy in the farm shop, while Jules and Sharpie really brought the place to life.

By 9.30am, we were all up and trading. There was a terrific atmosphere in the barn – the gas heaters gave it a welcome warmth, the stalls looked fantastic and if you looked into one of the loose boxes, you could see a mother suckling eight of her newly born piglets. People queued up for a cup of hot, freshly roasted coffee and warmed their hands as they chatted. Others wandered from stall to stall tasting the spicy chutneys, marvelling at the freshly made cakes and filling their carrier bags with fish, the best veg of the season or a chunk of cheese from the rounds piled up like sculptures on one of the trestle tables. It's the kind of shopping experience I love: an expedition that can result in a great Saturday lunch, that's all about finding ingredients that ooze perfection and lets you choose a little bit of what you fancy. The art is creating the perfect balance of tastes and textures. When you get it right, these are the meals that don't need cooking, just unwrapping, and you're ready to get stuck in. They're great for a lazy afternoon picnic in the park or to welcome a gathering of hungry mates. It could be as simple as some slices of local free range ham, a warm crusty loaf, a vibrant bunch of the freshest, punchiest rocket; or a dynamite cup of homemade soup, organic pâté or a ripe cheese at its peak. I think it's the key to farmers' market shopping and makes me think of how it must have been in the old days, when our parents used to go out and shop for each meal, every day, based on what looked good at the grocer's and the butcher's.

Back outside, Jamie said a few well-chosen words, rather than smash champagne against the shop wall (well, it's not a ship, and those walls took a lot of work to build) or cut a ribbon, to a warm round of applause and many beaming faces. Over the hours that followed, more people arrived, the tills became busy and the farm had never seemed so alive.

At the end of the day we were all ready to drop but before I knew it we were all down the pub. There were a ton of us to get over there and, in desperation for a pint, we piled eight lads into the back of the freezer truck. We shut the doors and it was pitch black inside but they still managed to drink a bottle of champagne on the way. Eventually about twenty-five of us turned up at the little local and we were ready to celebrate. We stayed the whole evening. Michaela and I played the piano and the guitar got passed around for a good old-fashioned sing-song. It was great to get together with everyone who had helped out that day and finish it off in high spirits. At last the shop was up and running, and the first day had been a triumph.

For the weeks that followed, we stuck to our hectic schedule of farmers' markets. We prepped our produce, set up and sold at our pitches and, on most occasions, returned to the farm frozen stiff. All the while we were hoping that business would pick up substantially, we'd do well in the shop and online and start paying off the heavy deficit with some hard-earned profit. We'd also added a new sausage to The Essex Pig Company repertoire. Spicy Lamb Sausage was a recipe Rick tried out, initially with some left-over Norfolk Horn Lamb (a rare breed) from the farm shop opening, which he mixed with a little rusk and some organic spices. They are magnificent! As usual, besides the sausage-making and farmers' markets, there was also the daily running of the farm to attend to and the animals to feed.

I'd had rather a good idea to give the pigs even more variety in their diet than they were gleaning from the woodland, and to make their dry feed go further. I decided to buy some vegetables in bulk from a local farmer who was advertising them cheap. As I mentioned earlier, pigs love fresh produce in their feed and will reward you for it in the quality of their meat. The trouble was that this time, I think I went a bit overboard. I ordered 20 tons of carrots and waited for them to be delivered. The day they arrived, I couldn't believe it. Have you ever seen what 20 tons of carrots looks like? Nor had I, until I saw what appeared to be an orange mountain that had been dropped on the farm. The pigs, however, were ecstatic – they went mad for these new crunchy goodies and couldn't seem to get enough of them. After a few days, however, I began to notice some strange side-effects. The pigs' poo turned bright orange and I was sure the pigs themselves were changing colour too, especially the Tamworths. Now I know that Tamworths are ginger anyway but they were starting to look like Tamworths with a tan. I decided that I should cut down the amount of carrots I gave the pigs each day and rationed them until they looked normal again.

Before we knew it, February was upon us. As part of my new enterprising way of thinking, I decided we should try and cash in on Valentine's Day. Rick, Asa and I made tons of our popular Love Sausage, and Michaela and I spent the day trading in Sainsbury's car park at the Norwich farmers' market. Poor Michaela, it probably wasn't the most romantic Valentine's Day she'd ever spent, and unfortunately we didn't sell much either. It was a cold wet day that started off icy when we got up at six and, as the hours passed, it continued cold and drizzly. The miserable weather kept the shoppers away – instead of wandering around, browsing at the market stalls, I saw most people dash into the superstore, run back under their brollies and head straight off in their cars. I couldn't blame them. But we stood it out just in case the weather cleared and business picked up. By the end of trading, we were so tired and cold from being up so early and getting soaked to the skin that we cancelled our Valentine's meal out that evening. I did manage to buy my girl a bunch of flowers, though, so I didn't end up in too much trouble.

Plans to be a cowboy

Back on the farm, I had an urge to start looking at buying cattle. I love cows – there is something so calm and settling about them; they have placid temperaments, big doe eyes and an inquisitive nature. Keeping cattle was something I was planning for the following year but, in the meantime, I was keen to learn about breeds and find the right cows for our farm. As with any animal, it's important to get the right breed for the right

BELOW Opening day for our farm shop was a great success. Here's me looking just the picture in my specially made Essex Pig Company T-shirt!

environment, whether you are buying a house pet or livestock for a farm. You should think about the space you have, what kind of time you have to look after the animal and what methods of doing so you prefer. Besides, cows are quite a big step up from the other animals we kept on the farm, in size alone. You can visit one of the big agricultural shows such as the Suffolk or the Royal and see Herefords, Shorthorns or Aberdeen Angus and as you get up close to them you can't help but think, 'Blimey, they're colossal!' Cows can be massive so you need to make sure you have enough room to keep them before you think about buying. Especially bulls. They're handsome, strong, muscular animals but wilful too. It's no longer necessary to keep a bull to breed cows any more – artificial insemination is an easy and popular option. You can make a phone call to select a breed, choose the bull you want and buy the semen. It is even possible to buy the semen from bulls who have been dead for up to thirty years, which is great if you are trying to preserve a rare breed. I think it's amazing.

But first things first. I was torn between several rare breeds, so I visited two local farms to check them out. The first was Harlow, the children's farm and home to many rare breeds where I had found the legendary Lady Dictator boar; the second was Wimpole Hall and Farm in Cambridgeshire, a National Trust house, whose farm was designed by Sir John Soane in 1794 and is still home to a variety of rare-breed animals today. Between the two places, I had a good look at all the cattle options and weighed up their qualities.

Back in the garden

Over the long winter months, most of the garden sinks into dormancy, so there is a break from the constant care and weeding of the other seasons. With the weather being so miserable, the last thing you want to do is spend hours outside in the vegetable patch. But as the snow passes and the ground thaws out, it's time to venture outside with the trusty old fork and start bringing it all back to life. There is still a lot going on even during those dead-looking, grey weeks; if you planted rhubarb last season, it should have started to shoot up in January and you may find yourself with some sturdy stems for early picking by February. And now is also the time for winter cabbages such as savoys, cavolo nero and kale to come into their own. They all have a lengthy growing period, so plant them in the late spring and early summer, and have a good harvest over the winter months. They are a tasty accompaniment to roast meat or pasta, or wonderful in a good, hearty, homemade soup. I like them boiled until just tender, tossed in a generous knob of creamy butter and seasoned with crunchy sea salt and black pepper. Simple. I love the savoy's crinkly leaves and the fact that winter cabbages are pretty frost resistant, giving you something green on your plate and in the garden at the bleakest time of year. They'll stand throughout the winter, so just cut off the mature heads as you fancy them. Many other brassicas can face up to the frost too, such as Brussels sprouts and broccoli and will serve the same purpose.

ABOVE **Soay sheep are hardy animals, able to endure the toughest weather and environments.**

I also plant some shallots. Sow rows of the bulbs, during the winter giving them space, and you'll be rewarded in the summer by lots of little onions growing around the bulbs you planted. What's more, the crop should keep on coming good until the autumn. Shallots are fantastic to use in all sorts of dishes – you can roast them along with your chicken and get a delicious accompaniment to your meat, or chop them and use as the base for sauces instead of a regular onion for a particularly wonderful sweetness, but if you're clever you'll resist the temptation to chop the lot and remember to keep a few of the best bulbs back to plant the following year.

Really and truly, there is not much to be done in the winter garden: plants are dormant and the frost does a good job of fighting any diseases lurking in the bare earth. Nature doesn't provide us with many wild foods in the winter months either, but there is one little gem that shines at this time of year: the rose hip. Despite popular opinion that autumn is the time to collect them, I find the best time to hunt for the bright scarlet berries of the dog rose is straight after a frost. Rather than killing them off, the frost freezes the water inside the plants, which expands and bursts the cell walls, giving the berries a softer, mushier texture that intensifies their flavour and makes them easier to prepare in the kitchen. The rose hip contains twenty times more vitamin C than any other fruit or vegetable and it makes sense that nature provided us with such a rich source at this time of the year. They can be used to make an old-fashioned syrup or to flavour a wide range of desserts, jellies and jams. There's not much to forage for at this time of year

Tips on Keeping Cattle

• **Dexter** The Dexter are like mini cows, compact and sturdy, which makes them easy to look after and brilliant if you don't have much space but want to keep a dual-purpose cow, good for both milk and excellent beef. For this reason, they're popular with smallholders. They are good-looking and have black or sometimes red coats. There can be a downside to the Dexter: I find they can occasionally be temperamental and therefore tricky to move. A neat way to describe them is a small cow with a big personality. But I could be biased; I once got my finger crushed by a cheeky Dexter as I tried to tickle her under the chin.

• **Shetland** Also a good size for small farms are Shetland cows. As the name suggests, they originally lived wild on

the Shetland Islands and have changed very little since. It comes as no surprise, then, that these black and white cows are inherently hardy, weathering most UK conditions well and able to live happily on a free-range diet of grazing and a little roughage when producing milk. They are bred for their excellent milk, which is creamy and rich in butterfat, as well as their meat, which is also of good quality.

• **Gloucester** This is a very rare breed, threatened with extinction, so worth preserving if possible. It is distinguishable by a white stripe up the back. A dual-purpose cow, the Gloucester beef yields coated in a thick layer of yellow fat, making it very tasty. Butchers seem to

favour white rather than yellow fat these days – maybe it looks better on their counter – but I find it delicious and buttery. Gloucester cows' milk is used for making Stinking Bishop, and Double Gloucester cheese.

• **White Parks** These are some of the most ancient native cattle, and are very handsome creatures with black markings that just tip the ears, tail and feet. Because of the way the cattle have been bred, they are healthy, adaptable animals that thrive outside and live long lives, producing calves until they are about fifteen years old. While most people think of White Parks as ornamental cows, they also produce amazing beef, with a strong and distinctive flavour.

• **Red Polls** These are East Anglian cattle, created in the nineteenth century by crossbreeding the Suffolk Dun and the Norfolk Horn, both of which are now extinct. Red Polls have lovely red glossy coats, are dual purpose and low maintenance, so very suited to my farming methods. They do well outside on a traditional free-range diet, have good temperaments and are therefore easy to handle. For these reasons, the Red Poll was once celebrated as a dual-purpose animal and was popular, but they are now a rare breed. What's more, I liked the idea that they originated in East Anglia, so, as with my Essex pigs, we would be supporting a local breed in its traditional home and producing quality beef. Eventually we will breed the cattle and keep up the numbers. I think I've found my cows!

but there is a wonderful compensation: the shooting season. We shoot in season with good reason – to preserve birds and allow them to replenish their stocks, for example, and if shooting is done carefully, within regulations and for food, I don't having anything against it. Wild meat is often better than farmed for a whole variety of reasons, from nutrition to welfare – a bird that's led a healthy, free life in the wild, eating a natural diet and following its instincts is obviously going to be a happier bird than a commercially reared, cooped-up, medicated and miserable chook, and much better eating because of it.

Shooting is permitted if you have the appropriate firearms licence and game licence, and only consider it if you are a decent shot. Shooting is humane when done accurately – wounding any animal rather than killing it is a serious thing that should be avoided at all costs. With all this in mind, you will probably be glad to hear that there is a plentiful supply of delicious and cheap game from good butchers and farmers' markets at this time of year. The dark and flavoursome meat of the pheasant, partridge, pigeon or grouse is really something else. Have it traditionally – roasted, with bread sauce and game chips – or try something fancy with fruit stuffings. Whatever you do, it will be fantastic. These birds are some of the best eating around. While you're thinking about game, don't forget rabbit and venison. The cold, dark barrenness of winter is compensated by these rich and nutritious meats.

Sunshine in a jar

In the absence of all that is fresh and fruity, it is jams, chutneys, pickles, jellies and compotes that I turn to at this time of year – preserves, in the real sense. In the shortest, darkest days of the year I love to see my winter cupboard filled with these wonderful glossy, brightly coloured jars. If you think about it, jamjars packed with berries, oranges and quinces, for example, are like little time capsules of summer – just what we need when it's chilly and the skies are grey. Open a jar of the best Seville orange marmalade, close your eyes, think back to summer and bring some zest to a slice of warm crusty bread.

My love of jams led me to visit the world-famous Tiptree of Essex, to learn more about how some of the best jams around are made and buy some stock for the farm shop. It was a real treat, because every product we sell in the shop, we insist we taste!

You know when you have arrived at the Tiptree jam factory because the smell as you pull up in the car park is just fantastic. That morning it cut through the chilly winter breeze and smelt sweetly of warm, ripe summer fruits and I couldn't wait to get inside. I was met by Mark Smith, who has the highly respected role of Tiptree Production Controller, who had agreed to show me around the factory.

Tiptree, I soon discovered, is a modern firm using modern production techniques while still retaining its traditional roots, methods and small-company ethos. You can buy some of their jams in the supermarket but it's very much a family-run business. Unlike most jam producers, for example, Tiptree refuse to buy in fruit concentrates. They have

OPPOSITE Tiptree preserves, made just over the border in Essex, are among the high-quality items we sell in our farm shop. The family-run firm has a traditional, hands-on approach, and we also use their fruit waste to feed to our lucky pigs.

their own farm, where they grow and harvest all of their fruit (apart from oranges, which obviously don't do well in our British climate – they import those). When the fruit arrives at the factory, it hits the production line where the peelers are all lined up. They could do much more of the cutting up and pulping of the fruit with machinery but for the majority of the tasks they stick with the ways that they have always done things. Once prepared, the fruit makes its way into large, stainless steel vats. That day, there was a vast amount of orange marmalade on the go, a warm, heady, thick soup of silky orange bubbling away, and a similar container of lush shiny blackberries that smelt so good, you felt as though you could just dive into it. It was like being in Willy Wonka's Chocolate Factory.

The people that work at Tiptree seemed to have been there forever. Some had been with the firm for twenty-five years and one gent I spoke to who'd been employed for a full ten years was still considered the new boy, the apprentice! He told me that when you're new, like him, you get teamed up with an old hand who keeps an eye on you and teaches you the company's ways. It did make me laugh. But it was refreshing to see a big company hold on to its roots and not give into the pressures of an accountant, who would probably recommend they make their jams from cheaper concentrates. Not only would they never compromise on taste in that way, but they couldn't produce their real corkers like that. I'm talking about the real traditional jams that Tiptree makes – the medlar jellies, the quince jam and the green fig jam. Delicious! Then there are the ones they make just for Fortnum & Mason; one of these has become a bit of a national institution.

Little Scarlet Conserve is a strawberry jam like no other. Tiptree cultivates the strawberries, which are very close to the wild strawberry variety – tiny but with superb flavour – on their farm, and they can hardly grow enough of them to make one whole consignment of jam at a time. They are the only company in the country to do so. Can you believe there is a waiting list to buy it? But so good is this stuff, with its intense, sweet flavour, that Ian Fleming wrote about the jam in his James Bond books. Amazingly, I managed to get hold of some jars to sell in the farm shop. They weren't cheap but worth it – just amazing! Mark came into his own when I got him talking about how Tiptree blends each jam just so. I didn't really realise that the process was such an art form, but it is far more like making olive oil or wine than our usual perception of a little old lady mixing up a jar or two for the Women's Institute.

A team of directors and controllers including Mark look after every detail – the colour, the texture, the blend of flavours and knowing exactly when to set the jam are all discussion points. Then a little something maybe added or changed here and there until a consensus is reached that it is perfect.

Mark let me take a peek in his stockroom. It was full of finished jars of jam ready to be labelled. Hundreds were lined up in rows as if they were colour coordinated and they looked beautiful: bright scarlet jars of strawberry and raspberry jams, others filled with glossy blackberries and black cherries and many more besides, all looking like rows and rows of jewels. Like I said before, to me, they were all like little time capsules of summer. Despite my childish glee at all the sweetness, I was there for a practical reason – to buy jam for the shop, which I did, but being a good old Essex boy, I managed to cut myself another deal in the process. After all, we were both Essex companies. . . I asked Mark what they did with their fruit waste. They usually gave it to a nearby farm but I thought it would be great to have some of it for my farm, so I offered to collect it in a van and have it transported to the farm, to feed my pigs. They would love it – a wonderful mix of pineapples, cherries, strawberries and all kinds of fruit pulp to mix with their feed. It would definitely make that £175 a ton of pig feed that I was getting through in a week go further, without the side-effects of too many carrots, I hoped.

As winter started to fade into spring, the weather started to slowly warm up, the grey skies lift and the pigs should have started to breed in the woodland. But Blaze, my favourite boar, didn't seem to be getting any of the females in pig. I couldn't believe it! He is such a rare Essex boar and they're thin on the ground, so I'd had high hopes of him continuing the line. Also, from the pigs' point of view, it's good for them to have litters – it's natural and lets the farmer know that everything is working properly. But part of the genetic make-up of the Essex is that they can have a low sperm count. Maybe it was a bit too early in the season to worry, but I called the vet up to run some scans, and he found that in fact none of the pigs were pregnant. I hoped that spring would come soon and with it, Essex piglets.

SPRING piglets galore

With the arrival of spring came a rush of excitement on the farm. After what had seemed like a never-ending winter, we all felt a much-needed boost of energy from the warmer, brighter weather, the sudden appearance of wild flowers and the promise of summer. It was wonderful to feel the sun on our backs again, and Asa and I marked the first day that felt as though spring had finally come with a bottle of beer and a walk in the woodland at the end of a busy afternoon. We gave the pigs a scratch, watched Cora run around despite her broken leg, spotted grass snakes and saw the sun go down through the trees. We sat against the base of a big old tree and thought about the months ahead. I was pleased with everything we'd achieved so far, with the farm shop up and trading, a smoothly running circuit of farmers' markets, and the whole place alive with animals. But, as you've probably guessed by now, a farmer's work is never done and there was no time to sit back and be pleased with ourselves. Now we had to start making sure that everything would be ticking over for another year, and that we had a decent amount of money coming in to keep us all going. We had a lot of hard graft to plan.

The farm awakens

The advent of the new season meant that there was spring-cleaning to be done on the farm and we started by mucking out the stalls where the pigs and piglets had lived that winter. We dug out all of the old straw and manure in the loose boxes and piled it in a heap for Russell, our neighbouring farmer, to use as fertiliser for his vegetables. We turned the pigs and piglets that had lived in the barn back out on to the fields and into the woodland, watching them trot around, grunting excitedly, their ears flapping as they chased each other. We got to work building new pens, tightening fences and fixing posts. The woodland was looking much clearer now that the pigs had been at work for a while and a lot of bracken and dead foliage had disappeared, although the pigs had carefully ignored trumpet after trumpet of bright yellow daffodils, which I could only imagine hadn't been good to eat, and the flowers bloomed triumphantly, bringing some spirit-lifting colour into the wood. In another patch of the woodland there were seedlings coming into their own and a sea of bluebells in an area which I planned to keep pig free. Parts of the farm needed a chance to regenerate, so pigs would be kept well away from those bits; in the fields that they'd already ploughed over and prepared, we put down grass seed, moving the pigs along to work their magic on another piece of land. It felt good to be working the land with the pigs, in the old-fashioned way that nature likes best.

As part of my spring-cleaning, I cleared out our Barbie-pink caravan one evening. We'd settled in a little too well over the winter and it was full of junk. Even though it was, I hoped, temporary, it was still our home for the foreseeable future and we could do with freshening it up a bit. Armed with a brand-new Hoover, I turned out the dogs, chucked out the unnecessary rubbish we'd collected over the winter months, cleaned everything down,

OPPOSITE Spring is a wonderful time of year – full of hope and life. It always gives me a thrill to see trees covered in blossom and plants nosing up through the earth. It's a time for preparing the ground for things that will reward you later in the year.

dusted and vacuumed, and got things ship-shape. I finished just as Michaela turned up at the caravan door, a shadowy figure now the sun had gone down. I could just see her hair blowing everywhere in the wind and her arms full of the laundry she'd bought back from the washing machine in the barn. The regular washing routine always seemed to interest the pigs, who never had to bother with anything so boring, and they would look fascinated by the crazy humans endlessly piling things in and out of the machine. Michaela was delighted with the job I'd done in the caravan, and we felt all comfortable and domestic – this place really was our home now.

Meanwhile the geese had entered into their laying period. It doesn't last long but the eggs are fantastic – they're so huge that you can't quite believe it when you collect your first one and it weighs almost half a pound. The dogs, who had lived first with us, then with the pigs, had now moved to the goose house and one morning Lady proudly presented us with the first lay of the season, carrying each egg gently in her mouth one at a time, without breaking a single one, and laying them down gently in the field for all to see. From then on, we had a constant supply of wonderful, rich eggs from the ducks and geese to sell in the farm shop. People sometimes picked up the outsized boxes of goose eggs saying, 'What on earth do I do with these?' – but generally they were a hit.

Fridays and Saturdays had begun to get busy in the shop and even during the week, trade was steady. Michaela had taken control of the place and she was great at organising the stock, pricing things up, making everything look nice and generally keeping it all ticking over and in good order. She enjoyed it so much that she decided she would work only part-time at her job in television, so that she could concentrate on running the farm shop. Everyone did their bit, taking their turn behind the counter, but it was Michaela who really made the shop run smoothly and got the till balanced at the end of a busy day. Because she was so good at it, I was a bit apprehensive of how we would fare when Michaela went to India for a couple of weeks, on an impromptu holiday with her sister. Rick, Asa, Lee, Lynn and I tried to keep things together while she was away but it was an enormous relief when Michaela got back, not just because she'd returned safely but because it had become obvious that she was only one really capable of making the shop work. And, of course, she thought we'd made a right mess of her set-up, getting all sorts of things wrong – but I just couldn't see it. All I knew was that it appeared far better and ran more smoothly when Michaela was around looking after things. She is a complete star and I don't know what I'd do without her.

As the weather picked up, so did our trade at the farmers' markets. Jade was even selling her own birdseed balls, made from a mixture of left-over pig fat and seeds. We'd give her a corner of our pitch at the local markets and she'd banter away, talking the talk and selling her birdseed balls like an old pro – she was great. We added the Cambridge market to our Essex Pig Company rounds every Sunday – having farmers and food producers in the main market square was a real hit with the locals. But then we discovered a new favourite. . .

Ally Pally Market

One crisp spring morning, Michaela and I got up early, loaded the van with a ton of sausages and headed down to north London for the Alexandra Palace Farmers' Market. The 6am start wasn't such a shock to the system now that the trees were turning green, the skies were clear and the sun, though weak, shone just enough to make us feel good. It was, however, quite a drive to the market and we weren't sure what to expect, so we braced ourselves for a long, tiring day. As we hitched up at the site, it looked beautiful. The other stall holders were setting up along a lovely tree-lined avenue and already people were milling around, drinking coffee from a pitch selling cups of freshly ground, foam-topped cappuccinos and teas. We unloaded the trailer and prepared our stall amongst a row of others selling all sorts of delicious produce from honey to buffalo mozzarella cheese, and from fantastic French bread to farm-fresh vegetables. There were about twenty-five of us in total. By ten o'clock the market had become a hubbub of activity and our stall seemed to be mobbed. To our complete amazement, we sold out of sausages completely by eleven thirty. We had no choice but to pack up after just one and a half hours of trading, with people still wanting to buy sausages and fellow stall holders eager to know if we'd come back again the following week. So much for a long and tiring day! We returned to the farm, chatting all the way in the van about the wonderful French

BELOW Geese are such territorial creatures that to begin with we had to keep them separate from the sheep.

ABOVE One of the loveliest sights on the farm in springtime is baby animals snuggling into their mothers for a good feed. My part in helping to produce this new generation makes me feel proud.

feel of the setting and how we thought we'd stumbled on the next Borough Market. It felt like a place about to boom in popularity and I wondered if I could persuade Jamie and Gennaro to set up stalls and really pull in the crowds.

Of course, following such a big hit, we were keen to trade at Alexandra Palace the following weekend and this time, we went more than prepared for the event. We took double the amount of sausages, some rare-breed lamb and some White Park beef from the Rare Breed Survival Trust. But again, we sold out completely in a couple of hours flat. This place was a treasure trove. I wasn't going to be available for the third week as I had a research trip to go on, so we decided that Rick would go to the market on his own. It wasn't a problem – Rick loves the markets and is a dab hand at them. Having heard our stories, he prepared the biggest load of sausages I'd ever seen and set off to London on the morning of the market with a van piled high with stock.

I followed him soon after with Rick's mate Lee, who had kindly offered to drive me to Stansted Airport. I was off to meet the men I called the Godfathers of Pig – Mr Vaughan Byrne and Mr Peter Gott. We were convening in Northern Ireland to talk about the Essex pig, the future of the breed and to see some of the few examples left in existence in Belfast Zoo. I couldn't wait.

The Essex pig, past and present

I was looking forward to seeing Vaughan again – he's a dead ringer for Terry Wogan and just as jovial, with a wicked sense of humour, a quick tongue, a photographic memory and an incredibly sharp mind. He's an absolute expert on animals, a walking encyclopedia. Vaughan can recite the year a particular rare-breed cow won a show, who bred her and the history of her bloodline, while talking at a million miles an hour, dropping in a side-splitting one-liner and supping on a pint of Guinness, all at the same time. Peter, my old friend and mentor, would be there too, with his warm Cumbrian charm, practical advice and nuggets of articulate wisdom. I felt as though I was going on a kind of pig pilgrimage and looked forward to learning even more about my favourite breed.

Vaughan and Peter met me as I arrived bleary eyed at Belfast Airport. Peter had just flown over from Liverpool and they were both waiting for me, wearing big smiles, as I walked through the gates. Vaughan was hilarious as usual, right from the outset. We climbed into his ramshackle old car; it was touch and go whether it would make it out of the airport car park and he strongly advised us to ask if we needed so much as a door or a window open. He wasn't being gentlemanly – his car was just so cranky that one false move on a wobbly window frame and it was in danger of falling apart! Luckily Vaughan got the motor going and gave us a guided tour of the sights of Northern Ireland we passed on the way to his sister's B&B, where Peter and I were staying. The countryside was beautiful. We saw Dexter cattle as we passed a craggy Irish hillside covered in heather, spectacular against the industrial Belfast skyline. Vaughan was responsible for bringing the Dexter cow back to Northern Ireland and also contributed in a substantial way in increasing the numbers of the Irish Moiled. In the same way, he was keen for me to breed up the Essex pig in East Anglia, its rightful home.

Once we arrived at the guest house, we grabbed a cuppa and started to chat about our favourite subject. . . you guessed it – the Essex pig. But before we got engrossed, I put in a call to Rick. It had been raining all day at Alexandra Palace and things were slow on the stall, he told me. Poor Rick, it must have been miserable, standing there on his own in a downpour. After our tea, I called Rick back to check that he was in good spirits at the end of trading. I was glad and amazed to hear that things had turned around. Rick was chuffed to announce that he had made a whopping profit that day. Despite the weather, he must have nearly sold out, even with his mountain of sausages.

That evening, Peter, Vaughan and I continued our piggy conversation in the pub. We ordered some food to slow down Vaughan's banter a bit, but couldn't believe our eyes when Peter's mixed grill turned up at the table. It was a meat feast of Desperate Dan proportions with a gammon on top of a steak, on top of kidneys, on top of sausages and so on and so on. It was outrageous! But it didn't stop any of us getting on with the subject in hand. We talked about how we could push forward the work of The Essex Pig

Society, which Vaughan had co-refounded in 1997, and we thought about how we could use it to promote a greater interest in bringing back the breed. I learnt a lot more about the history of the Essex pig from Vaughan, a real expert, and it was fascinating stuff.

Vaughan explained the chain of events that led to the amalgamation of the Essex and the Wessex pig to form the British Saddleback in 1967. The Common Agricultural Policy of 1956 was implemented to encourage food production after the war, he said, when food was a scarce commodity and farmers were paid to produce quantity over quality. This, of course, was a threat to rare breeds of all varieties, as the commercial pig became favoured to produce more and more, faster and faster, and the market for high-quality breeding stock dwindled. The commercial pig that did well on a commercial ration was favoured and many farmers stopped keeping traditional breeds of pig. Maintaining Essex and Wessex pigs, along with other rare breeds, was no longer financially viable under such modern methods, so the numbers diminished.

Vaughan had been the first farmer to keep Essex pigs in Ireland. In his youth, he had brought three sows from the Essex town of Brightwell to Northern Ireland, having recognised both their good looks and the excellent flavour of the pork they produced. But when the breeds were amalgamated, Vaughan, like many people at the time, thought that the amalgamation was compulsory and sold off his herd, which, no doubt, was turned into meat products. This was not uncommon. The last chairman of the Essex Pig Society at the time, Richard Muir, disagreed with the amalgamation to such a degree that he took all of his pigs to slaughter and wrote in the society's magazine that he would not be breeding any more Essex pigs, ever again. As people either sold off or amalgamated their perfectly good herds, the breed came into crisis and the numbers of Essex pigs in existence seriously declined. As I mentioned earlier, John Crowshaw was the only man to refuse to amalgamate his herd and the only farmer to keep pure Essex blood lines. It was possible, said Vaughan, to see Essex pigs until around 1974, when the last remaining herds became rare and extremely hard to track down.

Over twenty years later, in 1995, Vaughan told me that a chap called Ian Witney came to see him with the idea of resurrecting the breed and the Essex Pig Society. Vaughan had always loved the Essex pig; they were the first pigs that he had kept and, in his own words, he felt 'quite emotional about them'. Vaughan and Ian were able to use the pure blood lines that John Crowshaw had saved to breed pure Essex pigs. They concentrated on breeding these up and realised that they could continue and carry on the work that John Crowshaw had started. They used Glasscoat boars and set up a breeding programme with help from Mr John Stronge, the then-manager of Belfast Zoo. John Stronge was fundamental in the scheme as was Stephen Booth (my mentor from Cheshire), who was in the background and very much like their man in Havana, according to Vaughan, sourcing and placing the Glasscoat boars where they were needed.

OPPOSITE Peter Gott (top left) and Vaughan Byrne (bottom left) are experts on rare breeds and were generosity itself to me with their time and knowledge. I couldn't have wished for two better mentors.

During this period, Vaughan wrote an article for the Rare Breed Survival Trust's magazine. It was a history of the Essex pig that he had put together himself, following 40 years of personal research. At the end of the article, he wrote that he thought it would be a great idea if someone did something to save the breed and hinted that the Essex Pig Society had been re-formed. Someone in the Rare Breed Survival Trust sent out an appeal for Essex pig memorabilia and he was inundated with the stuff, because it was a well-thought-of pig, especially in East Anglia and the county of Essex. This proved that there was still a huge interest in the breed. The society gathered momentum and soon became a couple of hundred members strong.

The society today is primarily made up of pig enthusiasts. Peter, Vaughan and I couldn't help but wonder, as we got in another round from the bar, if there was more that it could be doing. We wanted to reach a wider audience and encourage people to start breeding up the Essex pig all over the country, with a core base in East Anglia, the traditional home of the pig.

So, you're probably wondering, why all the fuss over this particular breed of pig? There's something about it that inspires a deep affection. The Essex pig was traditionally kept for both its looks and its pork – as Vaughan says, 'it looks good both on and off the hook.' It's a pig with a fine skin for showing, a bit of a stunner with attractive black-and-white markings that are easy to fall in love with. The Essex is predominantly a black pig with some white markings, often with a white nose, a white saddle (the stripe which goes across its shoulders), white front feet and back feet, as well as a white tail and often a white dash on the forehead. These markings differ from the Wessex, which has no other white marks on its black body other than a white saddle. The Wessex characteristics harp back to the Large Black, and the Essex goes back to the Old English hog, so while they share a similar look, they have a very different genetic make-up.

As with most lop-eared pigs, the Essex are also very docile animals and the females are extremely good mothers. The sows breed until they are around eight or nine years old and have large litters. In fact, Vaughan had one Essex pig who managed to produce 94 piglets in ten litters! – a great economic proposition for any farmer. As I have already mentioned, the Essex is also a hardy pig. Although it was bred in the relatively mild climate of East Anglia, it can quite happily survive climates as northerly as Inverness and as westerly as Northern Ireland, foraging for its own food. And the Essex doesn't need fancy housing either, just an ark made from a cheap material such as corrugated iron, meaning that farmers don't need to splash out on custom-built housing. One of the reasons that the Essex is so tough is that it changes its coat every year; because of overbreeding, the white commercial pig no longer does this – it has lost its hardiness and needs to be kept in an artificially warm environment. So, all in all, the Essex is a wonderful low-maintenance pig, with fantastic attributes and a great temperament. A winner all round.

OPPOSITE Essex pigs make great mothers, which is just as well when they can produce up to ten piglets per litter. These youngsters are about two months old.

The next day, Peter, Vaughan and I went to Belfast Zoo to see the Essex pigs that live there. We had a lot of laughs and a lot of fun that day and it was great to see the pigs in a sty within a state-of-the-art modern zoo, although I have to admit that there was also something sad about it. We passed all of the exotic animals such as rhinos, elephants and giraffes and then, all of a sudden, there were pigs. But that is what the Essex has come to: almost a relic of the past that needs to be preserved in a museum. It made me think of Vaughan's boar. He is a ripe old age, probably in his 90s in pig years, and Vaughan had become so attached to him that he let him have his day, as they say, and live out his natural life. The old boy is getting long-haired and going grey where he was once black, but he is a real rarity and a pig to treasure all the same.

Babies galore

Back on the farm in Suffolk, as if to confirm that spring had arrived, piglets were being born. The Middle White had a litter, as did a Tamworth and a wild boar – the piglets just kept on coming. But the best news was that the Tamworth and the wild boar had only been mated with Blaze, so he had done his job after all. The pigs had three black-and-white piglets each and although these litters were small, there was hope for Blaze yet. He was, after all, only a year old and might become more of a red-blooded boar with age. I was more than a bit relieved; Blaze was a good old boy and one with very important credentials in terms of his bloodline. If he hadn't pulled through, I would have to justify to myself, and everyone else, why he shouldn't be made into sausages.

Ethel was another sow to have piglets, this time in the woodland. She went off a few days before the birth and set about making a nest in a shady hollow beneath some trees. She gathered a mound of leaves and twigs by wandering to and fro, adding to her pile with hundreds of tiny mouthfuls that would have taken me hours to fetch in a wheelbarrow. Then bit by bit, she carefully spread them out and built up her nest on her chosen patch on the woodland floor. A few hours before the big event she tunnelled inside the nest, made herself comfortable and later gave birth to five piglets. We soon noticed that one had gone missing, but that's not unusual for pigs giving birth naturally; Ethel may have rolled over and crushed one of the newly borns, or it could have easily been taken by a fox – neither would have been out of the ordinary. The main thing was that the four that survived were great, healthy little piglets. How fantastic for them to come out of the nest the day they found their feet and to see a huge expanse of woodland. So much better than concrete walls. And they would get everything they needed from their mum and extra goodies from foraging out in the open. It was great to watch Ethel with her little ones – she trundled off on her own, her piglets in tow, and I could follow their tracks to see what they'd been up to. It was quite magical.

Spotting the wild boar-cross and her newly born piglets wasn't so easy – her brown

OPPOSITE While the pigs all have warm, dry accommodation on the farm, they prefer to make their own nests when they are due to farrow. Once the piglets are born, they stay close to their mothers.

coat was so well camouflaged in the woodland. When our curiosity got the better of us, we launched a proper full-scale search and eventually discovered that, like Ethel, she had made her own nest and had some sparky black-and-white piglets that were running around beside her. The wild boar and the Tamworth gave birth around the same time and they seemed to share their piglets and stick together in one large group in the woodland. It was lovely to see.

Not all of the new piglets and their mothers were able to live in the woodland. It just wasn't possible. Pigs need a lot of space and they generally like to stick with their own group, unless they have slowly been allowed to get used to one another. You should be able to introduce different pigs to each other in groups of twos and threes, as long as they have adequate room and it is a gentle process. But if you put one pig into a completely different herd of ten others, they will kill it if it feels new and strange to them. For that reason, farmers years ago would rub vinegar on the skins of different pigs, to mask their natural smell and supposedly allow the pigs to take to each other.

We put our pigs on various patches in the paddocks, the fields and the woodland, with the eventual aim that they would all roam the woods. Having made such progress with this plan, we were now working with the Forestry Commission, using the pigs to regenerate the land and keep farming and nature working in harmony. The farm owner would benefit financially and we got to keep the pigs in a fantastic habitat. I hoped that it was only a matter of time before we increased the amount of pigs we had in the woods.

I still needed to focus on breeding Essex pigs, however, and even though poor old Blaze had done his best, he wasn't doing the job quite fast enough. Infertility had become an inherent quality of the Essex boar as the breed declined, and the genetic gene pool was decreasing. As with any interbreeding, it was inevitable that negative traits would arise; it's nature's way of sending out a warning sign that something is wrong, to mark the close of a useful cycle of breeding. It spurred us on to do something about it, and fast.

I got in touch with a farm in Harlow and spoke to them about borrowing their Essex boar to breed up some more litters on my farm. Justin Hopwood happily agreed and a few days later I was on my way to Harlow in my trusty trailer to pick up one of the rarest boars in the country. As he was an Essex, they'd aptly named him Jason. They also had two other Essex females named Sharon and Tracy. Of course I got the joke, but they are such majestic animals, that I couldn't help but feel that the names didn't do them justice.

I remember driving back to Suffolk with this amazing creature in the trailer, knowing that the drivers of the cars that overtook me had no idea what I had in the back. Mum called my hands free as I was just on the outskirts of Harlow, saying, 'You didn't tell me you were local, why not stop by for a cup of tea?' but I couldn't really pop in for a chat with a great big boar in tow. I headed straight back to the farm, to get Jason into the courtyard and keep him away from the females. Meanwhile, Rick had moved Blaze into the big, open field with Jasper and the other Essex piglets. Poor old Blaze – it was the equivalent of being relegated to the kiddies' table at a dinner party.

We had no trouble getting Jason into his new home, despite the size of the chap, and it was interesting to watch as he immediately started to mark out his territory. He urinated everywhere to stamp out the smell of Blaze, and had a good snort around to acclimatise himself. We'd taken care to separate Jason from the sows and gilts (a female pig who is yet to have a litter) so that they could get used to each other and so that the females could be introduced to the boar. It was important that they come into his environment, rather than the other way round. So we introduced them slowly, for just a short time each day and separated them again – a traditional trick designed to build up interest and encourage mating. And it worked, but not entirely as planned. After the pigs had all spent some time together and were sent back to their own quarters, Jason smashed the gate down to get to the females one evening. You just can't stop a boar getting to the ladies when he wants to.

Shortly afterwards, I received another boar from Stephen Booth. He had kindly bred me up a pure Essex boar to bolster my breeding stock. Rick's mate Lee went to collect the chap and bring him back to the farm, and we put him in the dairy. Although he was still young, he was magnificent. Let's just say it was clear to see that he had all of the makings of a great boar. I could only hope that we'd have more piglets on the way as a result.

BELOW I was delighted when Ethel fell pregnant. She's one of our Lops and went on to produce five little piglets, one of whom mysteriously disappeared – perhaps to foxes.

Hog heaven

In the meantime, I had extremely happy pigs. My 5 tons of jam waste from Tiptree of Essex had arrived and the animals absolutely loved it. The waste had been delivered in a big skip on the back of a vast lorry one April afternoon by a skilful driver who managed to weave his lorry around the farm despite the vehicle's size. He tipped up the skip and poured the whole 5 tons of jammy sludge into a small shed with no roof, one of the outbuildings that was yet to be fully repaired.

To us, it was a big, cold, mushy soup of pulp, pips and peel that hadn't made it into the vats at Tiptree, and, although it smelt great, it looked to the human eye like a colossal pile of sick. But for the little porkers, it was a tasty multi-coloured dessert of many fruits: blackberries, raspberries, oranges, pineapples and strawberries, to guzzle every day after their feed.

Old Matt, who still came up to the farm from time to time when walking his dog and to help me feed the pigs, said that we just needed a big bowl of custard and we'd be away. Lucky pigs! Every day we scooped up big buckets full of the fruit and put it out for them and they adored it. We got through the whole 5 tons in no time and a good job too – it would probably have begun to ferment before too long and we'd have had a drunken herd on our hands. I also had 20 tons of spuds arrive around the same time, from the farmer who had sold me the mountain of carrots, and they more or less disappeared as well. It's incredible what a few pigs can nosh through. . . But, as Gennaro commented with a hungry look on his face when I told him about their new luxurious diet, the meat from the pigs would be so sweet.

The Essex Pig Company on its way

It was a source of enormous pride to me that the quality of our sausages and roasting joints was being appreciated. We had delicatessens calling us up, wanting to stock our products, as well as a steady stream of regular shoppers at the farmers' markets, the farm shop and online. I was also very excited about Moving Feasts, the company belonging to Linda and Meg who had so kindly helped me out at the BBC Festive Good Food Show at Earl's Court. They were planning to sell our sausages at the Glastonbury Festival later on in the year. In the meantime, I'd also conjured up a plan to get some more publicity for The Essex Pig Company.

Unlike my brother who's mad about West Ham, I know nothing about football, but I thought a sausage named after the Ipswich team would go down well at the local farmers' markets and with the Suffolk press. The Ipswich team are known as the Super Blues, so I thought that a sausage with a hint of blue cheese would be a tasty and appropriate mix. I devised a recipe combining our rare-breed sausage meat with Stilton and fresh garlic and

OPPOSITE **Raising good healthy animals is very satisfying, this Middle White cross British Lop is a great example.**

got in touch with the club. They invited me down one Saturday morning before a training session. I went into their kitchen where the team's breakfast was being cooked and fried up some samples for the boys to taste. They went mad for the sausage! The Super Blues were a great laugh and I even got a chance to see Simon Milton, one of the team's ex-players and an old mate of Asa's, who introduced me to the team. The guys presented me with a signed shirt, a lovely gesture, and I headed off feeling extremely pleased. Simon must have been cursing the next day when the lads lost their match! I hope all those sausages didn't weigh them down Nevertheless, it finally felt as though The Essex Pig Company was winning.

There was a lot of interest building up around The Essex Pig Company and the initial gamble of taking on the farm, trying to turn it around and create a business from scratch was finally starting to pay off. In the beginning I felt as though I was going out into the unknown and nobody really understood what I was trying to achieve but now people were seeing it happen, literally tasting the success, and all of a sudden it wasn't just me saying it would work – others were too and there seemed to be a snowball effect.

More money had started to come in as a result of this and a lot of hard work, but it always seemed to go straight out again. As we became busier, it cost us more to produce a larger quantity of sausages and bacon as well as carry more stock. We forever needed more bags, more sausage skins, more fuel, more feed, more of everything. The list was endless and swallowed up a hefty chunk of any profit. But at least there was enough left over to pay the bills. By May, it looked as though we would soon break even and could start paying back the dreaded deficit. It would have been great to take a wage but, in the

BELOW AND OPPOSITE It's not always the case that different groups get on together, but our pigs have shared the same fields since the beginning and seem to enjoy each other's company.

meantime, at least I had all of the sausages I could eat. I never thought the farm would make me a millionaire – I was just happy to sustain the way of life I had grown to love. Not many people set off to work in the morning across a misty field as they trundle off to feed the goats. I'd also met some amazing people and their generosity and kindness never ceased to amaze me.

There were two incidents in particular that stuck in my mind from that season. I remember meeting a lovely old boy called Mo, when he turned up at the farm on the day of the shop opening. I must have met and spoken to dozens of people that day, but he was a fascinating character who told me that he had some chickens for sale and that he was interested in rearing some large Black pigs. We got chatting and eventually I said I'd buy his chickens off him, to build up our stock. A few days later I took a trip to his traditional farm in the nearby Suffolk countryside. It was a sunny spring morning and we ended up chewing the fat on all sorts of subjects as he showed me round his land. He offered me his advice on relationships, human and pig, and before I knew it, I'd been there with Mo for hours. I picked up a lovely trio of Light Sussex hens and five other chickens a few days later and was speechless when Mo told me to put my wallet away. He and his wife had been talking and because Michaela and I were just starting out, they decided to give us the birds for free. What lovely people.

I'd also become mates with Jules and Sharpie, who had been such a hit at the farm shop opening, dishing out delicious samples of their jams and jellies – I'm a big fan of their products. I was curious when they told me that they had been working on some new recipes and amazed when they invited me over to Jules' house to make a new jam they had

concocted just for me. Yes – a jam, just for me! I was thrilled, and jumped into the van that morning and drove out into the sticks. Jules lives in a little old village in Suffolk that looks like it hasn't changed for years. Her home is the old post house, complete with a safe where the bonds would have been kept. It has a wonderful feel: homely, cosy and elegant. The kitchen is brilliantly designed, with modern appliances that worked seamlessly with the rustic, traditional furniture – a great place to get cooking. We picked a bright bunch of rhubarb from the garden, smashed up some ginger and started to make the jam in a big old pan (see p.212 for the recipe). I couldn't wait to taste it – the warm, glossy, crimson mixture looked amazing as we poured it into about 20 jars and I had to stop myself from tucking in with a big spoon before it set. When I did, I wasn't disappointed – it was absolutely splendid and I'm now the proud maker of my very own jam.

The wild larder is replenished

Back in my own kitchen, I was able to begin cooking with some of the wild foods that had started to pop up around the farm. Tons of wild garlic were weaving a line around the fence posts and I loved it. The leaves are just as pungent as the bulbs and taste great chopped up in a stir-fry or even when used to spice up a quick sarnie. I have to confess to chomping on a few leaves as I pick them, when I'm fixing a bit of fencing, but that's probably not to everyone's taste.

There was also wild watercress to be found. There are actually two types of watercress that are native to the UK: one has a dark green leaf and the other has a bronze sheen. I'm a fan of both, but the latter tends to be a hardier plant with a stronger, more peppery flavour. I gathered a great big bunch of the first kind, from the stream in the woods. But a word of warning – pick with caution and see my tips about wild food (see pages 176 and 177) for details. If you can't find watercress growing wild in a situation that seems safe for consumption, you can always have a go at growing your own, either on a window sill or outside. If you have a patch of garden or vegetable plot where you can dig a small trench, you're laughing. You can have great salads and make delicious soup within a month or so of planting at this time of year and if you're careful, your crop could last through the summer. Here's how to do it.

There are two ways to grow watercress in a garden: from plant or seed. The easiest way is to get out on to your patch in April/May time and dig a deep trench (preferably in a damp or shady spot) that's 20cm wide by 60cm long. Mix in a bucketful of manure or well-rotted compost, into the earth at the bottom of your trench and flood it with water. Now you can either plant 10cm shoots from good, healthy organic plants, or sprinkle in some seeds. Water your trench daily and your plants will quickly take root and establish. I've been lucky enough to start picking just four weeks after planting in the past. Remember that if you pick off the tops of your plants, you'll constantly encourage more new leaves to

OPPOSITE Producing your own food is fantastic, but finding it for free is even better. With everything bursting into blossom right on cue, we were confident of gathering lots of treats come the autumn.

grow, and to remove any flower heads as soon as they appear. Perfect!

Another green leafy favourite of mine is nettles. Now, these get a lot of bad press, quite understandably, from gardeners who inherit a stubborn patch of the weed. But one chap's nuisance is another's feast and I think they are fantastic to eat. Back in the autumn, Gennaro and I found an abundance of nettles all over the farm and he made some fantastic fritters (see page 204 for the recipe) with them, but spring is also a great time to raid the hedgerows for a new crop of bright green nettles. Remember to carry a pair of thick gardening gloves with you, because even though Gennaro is convinced that if you sing 'hello, I love you' to them, they will not sting you, I'm not.

Other treats to look out for are the wild mushrooms that crop up in springtime. While most of us traditionally associate fungi with autumn, spring is the time to hunt for morels, the St George (named because it commonly appears around 23 April, St George's Day) and the wonderfully named fairy ring champion. A word of warning, though – while the latter looks and tastes fantastic, my advice to novices would be to avoid the fairy ring champion. It has a deadly poisonous look-a-like which grows in a similar way and is found in the same environments, namely by forming rings in the short grass of pastures and lawns. Instead, stick to searching for the tasty St George and the black morel at this time of the year.

What better way to celebrate St George's Day than with a fantastic crop of British mushrooms to prepare for dinner? They are versatile and have a delicious flavour. You'll find them growing in rings at the grassy edges of woodland from April until May (unless

RIGHT & OPPOSITE As trees green up, wild flowers open their tightly curled buds and the woodland becomes a magical place, full of colour and promising lots of future treasure in the form of wild food.

Tips on Wild Food

• Wild watercress is a great treat that can often be found growing in streams. But to be safe, avoid picking from streams where sheep are grazing, as the stems of cress found here are likely to contain eggs of the liver fluke, which is extremely dangerous to humans as well as sheep.

• Avoid picking cress in streams running through fields that could have been sprayed with fertilisers or pesticides. And finally, remember to give your cress a thorough washing before you reach for the chopping board.

• Pick nettles no higher than eight inches high, for the best of the crop. They have tender young leaves and a better flavour than bigger plants.

• Wash and simmer the nettles gently in a little water for around 15 minutes; drain, chop finely, add a big knob of butter and some seasoning and they're lovely with a poached egg and a thick slice of toasted farmhouse bread.

• Although most mushrooms are gathered during the autumn, some varieties do appear in the spring. If you strike gold with a fruitful mushroom patch, revisit it several days later for a second batch. Most mushrooms will have regrown during this time.

• The best time to go mushroom picking is in the early hours of the morning, when it is cool. This way you'll beat your fellow man, the wild animals and creatures such as

maggots and insects from getting to the mushrooms before you do.

• If you want to dry some of your mushrooms, keep the best of the crop you have gathered for the purpose. Give them a thorough wash, making sure that they are clean, free of insects, maggots and bits of leaf and twig. Pat them with a clean cloth to get rid of any surface moisture and lay them out on a tray. You can place the tray on a window ledge or in an airing cupboard for several days (depending on the size of the mushrooms) until they are completely dried and have changed into smaller, shrivelled shapes. Put your dried mushrooms into airtight jars, where they will keep for months.

• Reconstitute dried mushrooms before you use them in your cooking by soaking them in a little water overnight.

• At this time of year, quantities of wild garlic can be found in the countryside, and were particularly plentiful in our wood. Wild garlic loves damp places, but grows everywhere it is allowed to. It is mainly a woodland plant and has large green leaves and white flowers on a long stalk. It is out and ready for eating from March to late May/early June. You will smell it before you see it! The leaves are just as pungent as the bulbs and taste great chopped up in a stir-fry or even when used to spice up a quick sandwich.

the weather is particularly cool, in which case they'll pop up a bit later). They grow between five and fifteen centimetres wide and have white or creamy coloured caps which roll underneath at the edges. When the mushrooms are mature, these caps become wavy, with edges that look slightly torn. They have matching white stems and if you turn the mushroom over, you'll see that they have plenty of gills that are tightly packed on the underside. To gather them, cut the mushrooms individually at the stem and give the caps a good brush or wipe with a clean cloth to remove any dirt. Although their growing season is short, the St George dries well and can also be stored for a little while in virgin olive oil.

Another mushroom that dries particularly well is the black morel. People often take one look these mushrooms with their knobbly, gnarled-looking caps and think they are so ugly that they must taste terrible, but they are absolutely delicious. You can often spot them growing in clusters alongside shrubs on grassy roadsides and on disused land. They have creamy white stalks and a cap that is mid-brown in colour and rises to a softly pointed tip, full of pits and ridges, a bit like a sea sponge. Because of this, they are prone to becoming a feeding ground for lice and maggots, so only pick ones that look insect-free and be sure to wash them carefully before use. I usually slice them in half to do this and give each half of the mushroom a good rinse under a running tap and a pat dry with a clean cloth. It's worth going to all this trouble because the black morel has an intense, heady flavour that's great for making sauces and goes brilliantly well with meat. And, like all of the hedgerow food, it's all for free!

The spring garden

Spring is a funny old time in the vegetable patch. We often think that because daffodils and snow drops are popping up and the sun is shining in between those April showers, it is time to pull in a big harvest from our vegetable garden. This is wishful thinking. Spring is a season when most vegetables awaken from dormancy and embark on a growth spurt. It's a time to sow and bring on seedlings and plants and a time to pray that there won't be a nasty late frost! For this reason, I like to make myself a cloche at this time of year, to safeguard new seedlings against the unpredictable British climate. This might sound a bit fiddly, but really, it's a doddle.

I find that a plastic sheet, weighted with heavy stones to keep it secure, is enough to germinate and bring on brand-new seedlings that are planted in the springtime. When they get larger, you can make a simple cloche using a few old bricks to create walls. You should then cover the top with glass or Perspex that can be weighted down with extra bricks to ensure it doesn't shatter or fly off in the wind. There are many elaborate designs for cloches and tunnels – I've tried and tested a few in my time, with varying degrees of success – but my advice would be to start off simple and just have fun experimenting. The most basic, ramshackle structure should be enough to warm up the earth and bring your

OPPOSITE **As we have only female sheep, there were no new lambs during our first spring on the farm.**

vegetables on to the next stage of growth while deterring birds and insects from eating your baby crop. I'm particularly fond of using cloches to protect my salad crops. Growing from seed might sound like a long, drawn-out process but I have to tell you that it is well worth the extra effort. It's so rewarding to produce something from start to finish, to be able to bring a crisp, fresh green lettuce on to your table that you've grown from scratch. It's a great feeling and will taste far more delicious than anything you pick up at the supermarket, and will be better for you. It won't have been washed in chlorine, for one thing. The process might sound a bit daunting but if you follow the instructions on the back of any pack, you really can't go to wrong. And it makes great financial sense too. After your initial outlay for seed, your food will come free courtesy of the garden. Why not sow asparagus, broad or French beans, chicory, lettuces, corn salad, radishes or rocket this spring, and look forward to some tasty fresh treats in the months to come? Get out there and get creative. You could even liven up a bare wall with a few rows of runner beans. Drill two batons of wood into the wall and staple chicken wire to them, follow the instructions on the seed packet and watch them climb. I've been doing this since I was a kid and it's great fun.

Apart from pigs...

Unfortunately, there are no remedies for protecting your vegetables from some pests. Rick went out to the vegetable patch one spring afternoon to see how the cabbages were, only to discover that they had all disappeared. The goats had jumped the fence to get at them. They were still running around, hopping through the wire to cause all sorts of mischief. They had stripped the bark off trees, head-butted the glass in the shop windows like angry punks on seeing their reflections, and had eaten everything in sight. I thought that another line of sturdy barbed wire around their field might help contain their anarchy, but after a day or two they found another way through. Once they'd made their way to the other side, they stood and looked at me like I was the crazy one. They're bonkers.

As for the sheep, springtime meant lambing season – but not for us. I hadn't yet got round to getting rams on to the farm for our Soays. As a constant reminder, I seemed to see spring lambs in every field, dotted all over the countryside, everywhere I went, and they looked like great fun. Never mind, I thought, another thing to add to the list for next year. But I had also heard some horror stories from my friend Josh, who had been busy helping his ewes give birth, right round the clock. They needed a lot of help, unlike pigs, and it sounded like exhausting work. I was pleased that I had chosen to keep Soays; being such a primitive breed, they are naturally hardy and pretty much look after themselves, even when lambing, and I thought about how great it would be to have lambs in the years to come.

OPPOSITE With its clean coat of paint and some curtains at the windows, the farmhouse looks pretty good from the outside, but the truth is that it needs a huge amount of work to make it habitable.

I also had my eye on some fantastic Red Poles (rare-breed cows), as I mentioned in the previous chapter, and also had plans to start a herd of cattle, maybe with some Irish Moiled, the kind that Vaughan Byrne helped save. I also hoped to get kittens on the farm, to live in the barn and keep the rat and mouse population at bay. I already had my poultry, my pigs, the goats and the sheep but it was part of my plan to build up the livestock and open the farm up to the public, so that they could visit, see and learn about the rare breeds and the natural habitats they live in. I imagined kids going on mini pig safaris in the woodland while their parents stocked up on goodies in the farm shop.

But for the time being, I was very busy all the time, with keeping things going on the farm, increasing the Essex pig population any way that I could and really building up The Essex Pig Company.

Full circle

By the end of spring, it had been a year since I had discovered and rented the farm and naturally, I started to reflect. I'd enjoyed every minute of the adventure. It had been a great journey but the amount of work that we'd put in made it feel like we'd been there for ten years. I looked back at photographs from the beginning of the project and I couldn't believe all that we had achieved in such a short space of time. To see the way the place looked before we started is amazing: it was a wilderness of weeds, broken-down buildings and sagging old fences. Now it's a functioning farm, thriving and busy, with its own shop, butchery and processing plant, and repaired outhouses and courtyards. Where there was once ancient, overgrown vegetation, there are fields with livestock grazing. The ever-growing family of animals seems happy here, as they flourish in their free-range lives, grazing or foraging or laying eggs. I like to think we're giving them the happiest time possible as naturally as possible and that, in turn, they help us work the land and provide us with exceptional produce that is as tasty as it is healthy.

In pursuit of my dream, I've certainly dealt with the good, the bad and the ugly, as well as the unexpected. I never realised at the start how much red tape would be involved in getting the place up and running. At first, I had rosy visions of clearing land and mending fences but it was great deal more complicated than that. Every step forward took hours of planning and applying and explaining. Even simple things such as getting water and electricity supplied to a caravan were a minefield, and the bigger things, such as the opening my own shop and learning how to produce my own sausages, took much longer than I'd anticipated.

Then there were the problems I'd never dreamed of – I'd always thought that breeding up the pigs would be a simple matter but it turned out that getting pigs to mate is not a natural given, but something that can be quite tricky. I'd underestimated the intelligence of my animals and how many hours I would spend chasing escaping pigs and

OPPOSITE Jasper was without doubt one of the characters on the farm. He especially enjoyed being petted by Micheala – and at times we were sure he thought he was a puppy!

goats. I certainly hadn't anticipated how quickly a fire can spread. Or imagined that I would find myself hand-rearing a piglet who slept in the caravan.

Of course there are things that I wished I'd done differently. In a perfect world, I'd have had the farm shop open months before we managed it, and put in a decent row of fencing that wasn't so wiggly! But all these things are part of the learning process and, when I think about it, I know that we did the best we could in the circumstances. It's easy to forget how new and difficult everything was when we were just starting. More seriously, I wished that we had some pure Essex piglets by now and I regretted having the deficit hanging over our heads. These things are obstacles that I still have to overcome but I'm confident that, with hard work and dedication, I can get round them in time. I believe so strongly in preserving the Essex pig that I'm sure my plans will come to fruition in the end.

Looking ahead

Despite all the setbacks, there is a great deal to be thankful for. I could never imagine going back to my life in the city, and I don't regret the move for a second. It's hard work but it's incredibly rewarding, every day is different and, for the first time in a long time, I feel back in touch with the movement of the seasons and the cycles of nature. I couldn't give that up now: I feel happier for it, and so do the people who've joined me here on the farm. I try not to get too rosy-spectacled about it, but it really is the life that seems to suit us best, despite the miserable cold winter mornings and the endless routine of feeding the animals and the bad times when there's sickness or death in the herd. It only takes one glorious day spent outside, or a walk through the woods to see the pigs happily foraging in the undergrowth to know it's all worth it.

The growth of the Essex Pig Company has been a source of great satisfaction to Rick and me. We know we've achieved a lot and we're proud of our products. The best times are seeing people's reactions when they eat our sausages, or reading the delighted emails from our mail-order customers, or welcoming the regulars back time and again for more of our pork. I appreciate the reception we get wherever we go, such as the lady in Norfolk who gave me a photo of her with her Essex pigs that she had bred in the 1950s. Wonderful! We've showed proud friends and family that, with a little of their help, we really could pull our crazy plan off.

We've had brilliant fun with fellow traders who are like an unseen army, telling a joke, helping each other out, and working with passion and resilience as they push forward the quality of British food production. I've been inspired by them, and I hope I've passed on the message – that good food is out there if you look for it, in the farmers' markets and food fairs, lovingly crafted and produced. It's a treat and it makes no sense at all to ignore it.

It's strange to think back to the earliest days when Rick and I camped out for weeks, taking our jungle showers. Now the farm is alive with Rick's family and I still can't believe that I have Asa and Michaela living on the farm with me. Since they've moved on-site, we've had the very best of times. I had always hoped that Michaela would join me, but I could never ask her to give up her London life and her career. It would have been wrong of me to ask her to make that choice – it was a decision she needed to make on her own. And, to my delight, she has. Together, with Rick, Lynn and family, Dolly, Old Matt and of course the invaluable help of our mentors, we've become a great team.

We don't know what the future will hold. Maybe we'll be able to buy the farm and do up the farmhouse – or maybe we'll decide to move on, buy another farm and start all over again from scratch. But I do know one thing for sure and that is that this is just the start of the adventure for us and The Essex Pig Company.

RECIPES

Pumpkin risotto

Serves 4–6

1.6 litres vegetable stock
5 tablespoons olive oil
1 onion, finely chopped
4 garlic cloves, crushed but left whole
1 celery stalk, finely chopped
1 rosemary branch
350g Arborio rice
1 glass white wine
1kg pumpkin, peeled, deseeded and cut into small cubes
50g unsalted butter
175g Parmesan cheese, freshly grated
Maldon salt and freshly ground black pepper

Put the stock in a saucepan and bring to the boil. Keep it at simmering point while you make the risotto.

Heat the olive oil in a large saucepan, add the onion, garlic, celery and rosemary and sweat until soft. Remove and discard the garlic cloves. Add the rice and stir well for about a minute. Then add the wine and let it evaporate over a medium heat, stirring all the time. Add the pumpkin cubes, together with a ladleful of the hot stock. Stir until the liquid has been absorbed by the rice, then add another ladleful of stock. Continue for about 20 minutes, until the rice and pumpkin are just cooked.

Remove from the heat and stir in the butter and Parmesan. Check the seasoning and serve immediately.

Lynn's roast goose with potato stuffing

Serves 6–8

4.5kg goose
Maldon sea salt and freshly ground black pepper

Potato stuffing

450g new potatoes, peeled
50g salt pork or smoked bacon, diced
1 medium onion, chopped
1 teaspoon chopped mixed herbs
225g sausage meat

Rub the skin of the goose well with salt and pepper and set aside.

Boil the potatoes whole for 15–20 minutes, until tender, then drain well. Mash them and keep warm.

Fry the salt pork or bacon on a low heat until the fat starts to run. Fry the onion and cook gently until softened but not coloured. Stir in the mash, herbs, sausage meat, salt, pepper and extra basil, marjoram, lemon thyme and parsley. Remove from heat.

Turn the oven down to 160°C / Gas mark 3, put the goose in and roast for about 2 hours. You will know it is cooked when a leg breaks off easily. Give the bird a good baste during cooking and scoop out any excess fat, keeping it in reserve for your potatoes. Once the goose is done, remove from the oven, cover loosely with foil and leave to rest in a warm place until the remainder of the meal is ready.

Heat the oven to 220°C / Gas mark 7. Fill the cavity of the goose with the stuffing and place the bird on a rack set over a large roasting tray.

Pot-roast pork with apples, sage and leeks

Serves 4

olive oil
1 onion, finely sliced
1 garlic clove, crushed
3 Bramley or Granny Smith apples, peeled, cored and finely sliced
6 leeks, finely sliced
a bunch of sage leaves, torn
1 glass white wine
250ml vegetable or chicken stock
1.5kg boneless shoulder pork joint
2 dessertspoons crème fraîche
Maldon salt and freshly ground black pepper

Heat the oven to 180°C/Gas mark 4. Find a casserole large enough to hold the pork, with a tight-fitting lid. Heat it up well, then add the oil. Add the onion and garlic and fry until soft. Stir in the apples, leeks and sage, pour in the wine and stock, stir again and place the pork on top. Soak a piece of greaseproof paper in water and tuck it around the pork. Cover with the lid, place in the oven and cook for 2 hours. Remove the paper, take out the pork and rest on a warm plate. Stir the crème fraîche into the apple mixture, to make a thick sauce. Check seasoning and serve.

Essex pork sausages in red onion gravy

Serves 4

a little oil
12 pork sausages, weighing about 800g in total
1 red onion, finely sliced
1 garlic clove, chopped
1 tablespoon plain flour
250ml red wine
200ml chicken stock
leaves from a few sprigs of thyme
Maldon salt and freshly ground black pepper

Heat the oil in a pan, add the sausages and fry to give colour. Remove from the pan and set aside. Add a little oil to the pan and fry the onion until soft. Add the garlic, followed by the flour, and stir for a minute or two. Pour in the wine, stirring, then add the stock. Stir in the thyme and season. Put the sausages back in the pan, cover and simmer for 30 minutes, by which time the onion will have become soft, making a rich gravy. Taste and serve.

Classic pork sausage

500g minced pork

500g diced pork (5mm cubes)

50g toasted breadcrumbs (2 to 3 slices)

2 teaspoons sea salt

2 teaspoons cracked black pepper

Sausage skins (available from all good butchers, ask for enough to make 15-20 large sausages)

Place the minced and diced pork in a large bowl with the breadcrumbs, salt and pepper and mix together well.

Take your sausage skins and rinse them in water. Push a metal funnel into the end of one skin and tie a knot in the other end. Push the meat mixture through the funnel using the handle of a wooden spoon (make sure this can pass right through the funnel). Keep pushing meat through the tube, easing it down with your hands, until you have the size of sausage you want. Then twist the skin, tie a knot and cut it off. Repeat the process until you have filled all the skins. This may seem laborious at first but you will get into it.

To cook your sausages either fry in a hot pan with a little olive oil or for about 10–15 minutes or in a pre-heated oven 180°C/Gas mark 4 for about 30 minutes.

An important thing to remember about homemade sausages is that without preservatives they will only stay fresh for 2 days, so eat them very quickly.

The great thing about sausages is that you can experiment with the filling. Why not try adding finely chopped fresh chillies; herbs such as basil, marjoram or thyme; finely chopped garlic; spices such as nutmeg, chilli, cumin and coriander.

Sirloin steak marinated with mixed herbs

Serves 4

a handful of mixed herbs, such as lemon thyme, rosemary or bay
grated zest 1 lemon
1 garlic clove, chopped
3 tablespoons olive oil
Maldon salt and freshly ground black pepper
4 sirloin steaks

Chop the herbs and put them into a large polythene bag with the lemon zest, garlic, olive oil and seasoning. Add the steaks, seal the bag and leave to marinate for at least 2 hours and up to 24 hours.

Brush a frying pan with a little oil. Heat until very hot. Add the steaks. Fry the steaks according to how you like them: $1\,^1/_2$ minutes each side for a rare steak; 2 minutes for medium; $2\,^1/_2$ minutes for well done.

Nettle fritters

Serves 4

500g nettle tips
4 tablespoons plain flour
4 eggs
2 tablespoons Parmesan cheese, freshly grated
Maldon salt and freshly ground black pepper
120ml olive oil

Wash the nettle tips well, then blanch them in boiling salted water for 2 minutes. Drain and refresh in cold water. This improves the colour and the flavour. Drain again and squeeze out the excess water. Mix the nettles with the flour, eggs, Parmesan and a little seasoning.

Heat the oil in a frying pan and use a dessert spoon to drop the mixture into the pan i.e. one spoonful per fritter, frying a few at a time and turning them over when golden. Drain on kitchen paper, season and serve.

Apple and blackberry crumble

Serves 4–6

150g plain flour
1/2 teaspoon baking powder
100g unsalted butter
125g light muscovado sugar
75g muesli
3 Bramley apples, peeled, cored and finely sliced
200g blackberries
100g caster sugar

Heat the oven to 190°C/Gas mark 5. Put the flour and baking powder into a bowl and rub in the butter with your fingertips. Stir in the muscovado sugar and the muesli.

Mix the apples with the blackberries and caster sugar and place in a 1.5 litre/2 pint deep ovenproof dish, about 1.2 litres in capacity. Spread the crumble mixture on top and bake for 30 minutes, until lightly browned on top and bubbling underneath.

Chocolate chunk oat cookies

Makes about 30

150g unsalted butter
230g light soft brown sugar
1 egg
2 teaspoons vanilla extract
grated zest 1 orange
a pinch of salt
175g good-quality plain chocolate, at least 65 per cent cocoa solids, cut into chunks
230g rolled oats

Heat the oven to 180°C/Gas mark 4. In a large bowl, cream the butter with the sugar until light and fluffy. Beat in the egg and vanilla, then mix in the orange zest, salt and chocolate chunks. Fold in the oats.
Roll the mixture into walnut-sized balls and place on 2 baking sheets lined with baking parchment, squashing them slightly with your hand and spacing them well apart. Bake for about 15 minutes, until the cookies are golden around the edges. Remove from the oven, rest for a few minutes, then transfer to a wire rack to cool.

Cottage loaf

Makes 1 large loaf

500g strong white flour
1 sachet Easyblend yeast
2 teaspoons salt
250ml lukewarm water
2 tablespoons olive oil

Put the flour in a bowl, mix in the yeast and salt and make a well in the centre. Pour in half the water with the oil. Mix together, gradually incorporating the flour and adding the remaining water as needed, until you have a soft but not sticky dough.

Turn the dough out on to a lightly floured work surface and knead until soft, shiny and elastic – this will take around 10 minutes of arm power. Add a little more water if the dough is too dry or a little more flour if it is too sticky.

Put the dough into a clean, oiled bowl and cover with a tea towel. Leave in a warm place for about 50 minutes, until doubled in size. Knock back the risen dough and cut off a third of it, then shape both pieces into balls. Place the smaller piece on top of the larger one and plunge 2 fingers into the centre to join them together. Place on a floured baking sheet and cover with a tea towel, then leave in a warm place until doubled in size.

Meanwhile, heat the oven to 220°C/Gas mark 7. When the loaf has risen, dust it lightly with flour and bake for 45 minutes, or until it is browned and sounds hollow when tapped underneath. Transfer to a wire rack and leave to cool.

Flat bread

Makes 8

500g strong white flour
1 sachet Easyblend yeast
2 teaspoons salt
3 teaspoons cumin seeds, ground
250ml lukewarm water
1 tablespoon olive oil

Put the flour in a bowl, mix in the yeast, salt and cumin and make a well in the centre. Pour in half the water with the oil. Mix together, gradually incorporating the flour and adding the remaining water as needed, until you have a soft but not sticky dough. Turn the dough out on to a lightly floured work surface and knead until soft, shiny and elastic – this will take around 10 minutes of arm power. Add a little more water if the dough is too dry or a little more flour if it is too sticky.

Put the dough into a clean, oiled bowl and cover with a tea towel. Leave in a warm place for about 50 minutes, until doubled in size. Knock back the risen dough and divide it into 8 pieces. On a floured surface, roll each piece into a 20cm round.

Heat a dry heavy-based frying pan or flat griddle and cook the breads over a medium heat for about 2 minutes, until golden brown on both sides, flipping them over every few minutes. You can stack them and wrap in a tea towel to keep warm until they are all cooked.

Horseradish sauce

Serves 4

1/2 horseradish root
200g crème fraîche
Maldon salt and freshly ground black pepper

Peel the horseradish and grate it finely, being very careful as the strong vapour can affect your eyes and nose. Mix with the crème fraîche and season to taste.

Red tomato chutney

Makes about 2kg

3kg ripe tomatoes, skinned, deseeded and chopped
500g onions, finely chopped
25g salt
2 teaspoons paprika
a pinch of cayenne pepper
300ml distilled vinegar
250g raisins or chopped dates
400g granulated sugar

Put the tomatoes and onions in a large saucepan and cook over a low heat until pulpy. Add the salt, spices, half the vinegar and the raisins or dates and simmer for 40 minutes.

Stir in the sugar and the remaining vinegar; this helps to keep the deep red colour. Cook over a low heat, stirring occasionally, until the mixture is thick and all the excess liquid has evaporated – this will take about 20 minutes.

Pot the chutney in warm, sterilised jars (see Note below) and seal with vinegar-proof (i.e. plastic-coated) lids. The chutney should keep for a year in a cool, dark place; store in the fridge, eat within a month of opening.

Note
To sterilise jars, wash them in hot water, then place on a baking sheet and leave in a low oven to dry. Alternatively, you can put them through a dishwasher cycle.

Jules, Sharpie and Jimmy's hot rhubarb and ginger jam

Makes about 1kg. This delicious jam is not a 'set' jam, but has a smooth, slightly runny texture.

1kg rhubarb, cut into 2cm pieces
750g granulated sugar
grated zest 1 lemon
1 tablespoon ginger juice (squeeze fresh ginger root in a garlic press)
3 Thai chillies, deseeded and finely chopped
2 tablespoons lemon juice

Put the rhubarb, sugar, lemon zest, ginger juice and chillies into a preserving pan and leave for 2–3 hours. This will draw the liquid out of the rhubarb, so there's no need to add water – otherwise you could end up with soup!

Put the pan over a low heat and heat gently until the sugar has dissolved. Then (and only then) turn up the heat. Add the lemon juice and boil rapidly, stirring occasionally, until setting point is reached – 104.5°C on a sugar thermometer. (If you don't have a sugar thermometer, drop $1/_2$ teaspoon of the jam on to a chilled saucer and leave for a minute until it is cold, then push gently with your finger; if it wrinkles, the jam is ready.)

Spoon the mixture into hot sterilised jars (see page 211) and seal. The jam should keep for 4–6 months in a cool, dark place; store in the fridge once opened.

Lemon curd

Makes 450–500g

2 large eggs
115g unsalted butter, diced
115g caster sugar
grated zest and juice 3 lemons

Mix all the ingredients together in a heatproof bowl and place over a pan of gently simmering water, making sure the water doesn't touch the base of the bowl. Cook, stirring frequently, for 30–45 minutes, until the mixture is thick enough to coat the back of the spoon. Be careful not to let it boil or it will curdle.

Remove from the heat and strain the curd through a sieve into a bowl. Spoon into sterilised jars (see page 211) and seal. The lemon curd should keep for 1 month. Store in the fridge.

Elderflower cordial

Makes 750ml

6–8 heads of elderflower (avoid ones growing near a busy road)
575ml water
450g caster sugar
2 teaspoons citric acid
juice and zest 1 lemon

Tap the elderflower heads gently on a work surface to rid them of any dust or insects, then put them into a large bowl.

Bring the sugar and water slowly to the boil in a pan, stirring until the sugar dissolves. Remove from the heat and pour over the elderflowers. Stir in the citric acid and the lemon juice and zest. Cover and leave for 24 hours to infuse.

Strain and pour into sterilised bottles (see page 211), then seal. The cordial should keep for a year in a cool, dark place; store in the fridge once opened. If serving as a drink, dilute to taste.

Further reading

Books

Grieve, Mrs M., Leyel, Mrs C., *A Modern Herbal*, Jonathan Cape, London, 1974.

Thear, K., (Ed.), Fraser, A., (Ed.), *The Complete Book of Raising Livestock And Poultry*, Pan Books, 1988.

Rodway, R., *Food From The Countryside*, Park Lane, 1992.

Hamlyn All Colour Kitchen Gardening – Practical advice for Growing over 150 Vegetables, Fruits and Herbs, Hamlyn, 1992

Richardson, R., *Country Wisdom: Over 400 Practical Ideas for a Natural Home and Garden,* Kyle Cathie, 1997.

Heiney, P., *Home Farm: A Practical Guide To The Good Life*, Dorling Kindersley, 1998.

Don, M., Don,S., *Fork to Fork,* Conran Octopus,1999

Jordan, P., *The Mushroom Guide And Identifier – The Ultimate Guide to Identifying, Picking and Using Mushrooms*, Anness Publishing, 2000.

Wiseman, J., *The Pig: A British History*, Gerald Duckworth & Co, 2000.

McVicar, Jekka, *New Book of Herbs*, Dorling Kindersley, London, 2002.

Seymour, J., *The New Complete Book Of Self-Sufficiency: The Classic Guide For Realists And Dreamers*, Dorling Kindersley, London, 2002.

Erlandson, K., *Home Smoking and Curing*, Ebury Press, London, 2003.

Magazines

Country Smallholding Magazine (Buriton House, Station Road, Newport, Saffron Walden, Essex CB11 3PL) www.smallholding.com

The Smallholder (Hook House, Hook Road, Wimblington, March, Camb PE15 0QL) www.smallholder.co.uk

Useful addresses

www.essexpigcompany.com

Below are website addresses for farmers' markets located around the country:

www.farmersmarkets.net

London	www.lfm.org.uk
Hampshire	www.hampshirefarmersmarkets.co.uk
Gloucestershire	www.gafm.org
Monmouthshire	www.monmouthshire.gov.uk/food/farmersmarket.html
Scotland	www.scottishfarmersmarkets.co.uk
Wales	www.farmersmarketsinwales.co.uk
Ireland	www.irelandmarkets.com

Suppliers

Asco Butchers Sundries
(Sausage skins)
01440 710 060

Atlantic
(Animal/farming equipment)
The Old Mill, Earsham, Bungay
Suffolk NR35 2TQ

Natural Casting Company Ltd
(Sausage skins)
PO Box 133
Farnham GU10 5EB
01252 850454

Contacts

BPA (British Pig Association)
Trumpington Mews
40B High Street, Trumpington
Cambridge CB2 2LS

Compassion in World Farming
Charles House. 5A Charles Street,
Petersfield, Hampshire GU32 3EH
01730 264208
www.ciwf.co.uk

DEFRA (Department for the
Environment, Food and Rural Affairs)
Nobel House
17 Smith Aquare
London SW1P 3JR
www.defra.gov.uk

Henry Doubleday Research Association
Ryton Organic Gardens
Ryton-on Dunsmore
Coventry CV8 3LG
02476 303517
www.hdra.org.uk

National Cattle Association
60 Kenilworth Road
Leamington Spa
Warwickshire CV32 6JY
01926 889965

National Sheep Association
The Sheep Centre, Malvern
Worcestershire WR13 6PH
01684 892661

The Poultry Club
30 Grosvenor Road
Frampton
Boston
Lincolnshire PE20 1DB
01205 724081
www.poultryclub.org

Rare Breed Survival Trust
National Agricultural Centre
Stoneleigh Park
Warwickshire CV8 2LG
02476 696 551
www.rare-breeds.com

The Soil Association
86 Colston Street
Bristol BS1 5BB
0117 929 0661
www.soilassociation.og

Index

Acknowledgements

Dedicated to John Crowshaw

With many thanks to my darling Michaela; Asa; Rick, Lynn & the family; Lee; Peter Gott; Steven Booth for the breeding line; Vaughan Byrne; Anthony Carter; Mark Cooper; Simon Day; little Dave; Chris Terry for all his wonderful photographs; Matt & Carly; Des the hippy & Anna; Matt & Dolly; Andy Slade for dressing up as a chicken; my mum & dad; my brother Danny; my three cousins Faye, Amy & Beth; Jamie & Jules; Adi for selling loads of bacon; Stu & everyone at Bizerba; Louise Holland; John Dewar; Sam Scott-Jeffries and everyone at Ebury – special thanks to Lesley for not stressing out.

The Publishers would like to thank the National Trust for their cooperation during the photography at Wimpole Home Farm, Cambridgeshire.

Managing Editor: Lesley McOwan; Editorial Consultants: Sam Scott-Jeffries, Kirsty Fowkes and Trish Burgess; Design: Geoff Borin and Two Associates; Production: Antony Heller.

1 3 5 7 9 10 8 6 4 2. Copyright © Jimmy Doherty 2004. Jimmy Doherty has asserted his moral right to be identified as the author of this work in accordance with the Copyright, Design and Patents Act 1988. Photographs © Chris Terry 2004, except pages 46 and 207 © Getty Images. With the exception of the images on pages 46 and 207, Chris Terry has asserted his right to be identified as the photographer of the photographic material. All rights reserved. No part of this publication may be reproduced, stored in a retrieval system, or transmitted in any form by means, electronic, mechanical, photocopying, recording or otherwise, without the prior permission of the copyright owner. First published in the United Kingdom in 2004 by Ebury Press, Random House UK Ltd. Random House, 20 Vauxhall Bridge Road, London SW1V 2SA. Random House Australia (Pty) Ltd, 20 Alfred Street, Milsons Point, Sydney, New South Wales 2061, Australia. Random House New Zealand Ltd, 18 Poland Road, Glenfield, Auckland 10, New Zealand. Random House (Pty) Ltd, Endulini, 5A Jubilee Road, Parktown 2193, South Africa. Random House UK Ltd. Reg. No. 954009 www.randomhouse.co.uk. A CIP catalogue record for this book is available from the British Library. Papers used by Ebury Press are natural, recyclable products made from wood grown in sustainable forests. ISBN 0091897858. Printed and bound by Appl Druck Wemding, Germany.